What Every Teacher Should Know about Students with Special Needs

Promoting Success in the Classroom

Roger Pierangelo
George A. Giuliani

Research Press
2612 North Mattis Avenue
Champaign, Illinois 61822
www.researchpress.com

Printed in the United States of America.

9 8 7 6 5   09 10 11 12 13

Excerpts may be printed in connection with published reviews
in periodicals without express permission. No other part of this
book may be reproduced by any means without the written permission of the publisher.

Copies of this book may be ordered from Research Press at the
address given on the title page.

Composition by Jeff Helgesen
Cover design by Linda Brown, Positive I.D. Graphic Design, Inc.
Printed by Bang Printing

ISBN-13: 978–0–87822–467–8
ISBN-10: 0–87822–467–X
Library of Congress Catalog Number 00–109579

*To my wife, Jackie; my two children, Jacqueline
and Scott; my parents; my sister, Carol; and my
brother-in-law, George*

*In memory of Billy Smyth, a truly extraordinary
person and one of the most gifted men I have
ever known*

R. P.

*To my wife, Anita, and my two children,
Collin and Brittany, who give me the greatest life
imaginable*

G. A. G.

Contents

Acknowledgments

I wish to thank the students and parents of the Herricks Public Schools. It has been my pleasure to know and work with them for the past 28 years. Their insight, feedback, and support have been invaluable in the writing of this book. My gratitude also to Helen Firestone, who was instrumental in my career and always believed in me, and to John Okulski, a great individual and unique educator.

R. P.

I would like to thank the St. Joseph's College grant committee for their financial and personal support for my work on this book. Their continued encouragement is much appreciated. I am also grateful to St. Joseph's College itself, the greatest institution at which anyone could teach. They truly live by their motto, *esse non videri,* to be and not to seem. I also wish to express my appreciation to my colleagues in the Psychology Department. It is a pleasure to be a part of such a wonderful team. In addition, I thank my research assistant, Erin Bailey, whose efficiency, dedication, and organizational abilities helped so much in this book's completion. Perhaps most important, I want to express my gratitude to my parents, George and Carol Giuliani, who always made going to school a rewarding experience by giving me the self-confidence to believe I could succeed at anything I did.

G. A. G.

Our appreciation also goes to our friends at Research Press—especially to Ann Wendel and Karen Steiner—for their support and encouragement for this project.

R. P. and G. A. G.

Introduction

What Every Teacher Should Know about Students with Special Needs was written to provide you, the teacher of a child with a special need, with an easy-to-use reference on a myriad of special needs you may encounter in your career. Based on up-to-date research and over 40 years of combined classroom experience, this book gives you quick "tours" of each special need and then offers positive ways to help children with special needs reach their full potential. The dozens of practical strategies listed for each special need will not only help you guide these children to succeed in your classroom, they will also help other students learn to appreciate what these children *can* do, rather than focus on what they cannot. Children with special needs have much to teach all of us about diversity, patience, and compassion. Although gifted children are not "special needs" children according to the most common use of this term, their needs are special in the sense that they are unique. A look at giftedness and the needs of the gifted child rounds out this guide to teaching children with special needs.

Unless stated otherwise, when reporting incidence and other statistics we have used the information given in the revised fourth edition of the *Diagnostic and Statistical Manual of Mental Disorders* (American Psychiatric Association, 2000), known as the DSM-IV-TR. We also follow the DSM-IV-TR when we give names of specific disorders and discuss their diagnostic criteria.

Our Philosophy

As a teacher of a child with a special need, you must have additional knowledge and tools beyond the basics to use the 6 or 7 hours per day you spend with the child to the fullest. Indeed, these hours give you the opportunity to have a positive impact on the child's chances to succeed as an adult in our increasingly stressful and diverse society.

1

You may be thinking, "How do I individualize my approach for the child with a special need while balancing the needs of the rest of the children?" The answer is to be positive and, as alluded to earlier, to make the child's presence in your classroom benefit all your students. Certainly, many of the suggestions in this book are practical for all students no matter their abilities or needs. For example, working in small, cooperative groups of peers is a proven strategy for enhancing both academic learning and social skills development in other children. Consistent rewards, consequences, and classroom routines are also vital to eliciting appropriate behavior from other children. The list could go on and on. This continuity between accommodations for the child with a special need and the requirements of her classmates smoothes the path to better teaching and more learning for *each* student.

In addition, a positive prevention and intervention approach does more than create a positive learning atmosphere: It also builds self-esteem, empowers students to take more responsibility for their learning and behavior, and reinforces their strengths. We firmly believe that a positive, individualized approach builds a foundation of feelings of success and competency. In turn, this solid foundation opens the door to more learning and—most important—love of learning.

As you strive to create accommodations through which the child may feel successful and competent, keep in mind that this is not "spoiling" the child. The child with a special need has enough to deal with! For example, you may find it hard to allow a child with an emotional disability to do fewer math problems than his classmates. However, if the child becomes so overwhelmed that he cannot function, he learns nothing. Better to build level of effort and completion slowly than not to build it at all. Even a gifted child has emotional and social needs equal to or greater than those of his peers; it is important not to neglect these.

This book gives you insightful explanations and practical examples to help you understand the motives and needs of a child with special needs, and in turn help you to motivate the child. Choose and adapt the interventions you, in your professional judgment, feel will contribute most to the individual child's success. We hope that—whether you are a student teacher or seasoned veteran; special educator, regular classroom teacher, or college professor; administrator; or parent—this book will be the next best thing to having an expert by your side.

How to Use This Book

Each chapter in this book is devoted to one special need, and each chapter is divided into seven main sections:

+ *Definition:* Defines and describes the special need

- *Incidence:* Provides research-based statistics on the prevalence of the special need

- *Characteristics:* Specifies how the special need may manifest itself

- *Educational implications:* Gives a general overview of how the special need may impact the child's ability to learn and function in the classroom and of how you may meet the child's needs

- *Classroom management strategies:* The core of each chapter, providing classroom-tested, teacher-friendly tips for helping the child succeed in your classroom in the areas of academics, social skills development, behavior, and other applicable areas. The following general recommendations apply to all children, but especially to those with disabilities:

Approach the student without embarrassment, fear, or pity. Focus instead on the child's potential and gifts.

Avoid guessing what is wrong if you suspect a problem (either socially or academically). Be very direct, asking the child, "May I be of assistance?" instead of "May I help you?" The former helps the child focus on what he can do for himself, while the latter may encourage dependence.

Read and learn about the disability. It is important to know as much as possible and to try to be empathetic about what the child and family are experiencing.

Because each child is unique, make every effort to ensure that any academic goals set for the child match the child's intellectual ability and functional level.

A small but not insignificant point: Air-conditioning in the classroom in hot and humid weather makes the environment more conducive to learning for everyone.

- *Organizations:* A list of organizations, including Web sites and E-mail addresses where available, to which you and the child's family may turn for additional information and support. In addition to organizations specific to each chapter topic, two organizations are good sources of information for all:

ERIC Clearinghouse on Disabilities and Gifted Education
Council for Exceptional Children
1920 Association Drive
Reston, VA 22091–1589
800–328–0272 (voice/TTY)
Web site: www.cec.sped.org/ericec
E-mail: ericec@cec.sped.org

National Information Center for Children and Youth
  with Disabilities (NICHY)
P.O. Box 1492
Washington, DC 20013–1492
202–884–8200 (voice/TTY)
800–695–0285 (voice/TTY)
Web site: www.nichy.org
E-mail: nichy@aed.org

◆ *References and bibliography:* A list of the resources used to write
  the chapter and a handy guide to further reading

Special Education Legislation

To put the suggestions in this book in context, it is helpful to understand a bit about the current legislation under which special services
are provided. Public Law 94-142, the Education for All Handicapped
Children Act of 1975 (EHA), is the legislation that originally set forth
federal procedural safeguards for children with disabilities and their
parents, and outlined the foundation upon which current special education practices rest. Reauthorizations of and amendments to the EHA
have expanded the way special education services are provided, and to
whom. In 1990, the title of the law was changed to the Individuals
with Disabilities Education Act (IDEA). IDEA '97, the most recent
reauthorization and amendment of the act, lists the following specific
conditions as qualifying a child for special education services:

◆ Autism

◆ Deaf-blindness

◆ Deafness

◆ Emotional disturbance

◆ Hearing impairment

◆ Mental retardation

◆ Multiple disabilities

◆ Orthopedic impairment

◆ Other health impairment

◆ Specific learning disability

◆ Speech or language impairment

◆ Traumatic brain injury

◆ Visual impairment including blindness

Some children do not qualify for special services under IDEA, but they may be able to receive services under Section 504 of the Vocational Rehabilitation Act. Section 504, as it is commonly known, is a civil rights statute enacted in 1973 to prevent discrimination against all individuals with disabilities in programs receiving federal funds, including schools. Under this statute, a child may meet the criteria for special assistance. For example, even though a child with Attention-Deficit/Hyperactivity Disorder (AD/HD) may not be covered under federal law, that child may be entitled to receive classroom accommodations.

Special services under the IDEA are documented in an Individualized Educational Program (IEP). The IEP includes both short-term and long-term goals, along with specific information about how and where services will be provided. All students in special education are required to have an IEP designed to meet their needs. A Section 504 plan is a similar, though less rigorous, individual plan that spells out specific accommodations for the child with special needs who does not qualify for special services under federal law.

Assessment

Before receiving an IEP or a Section 504 plan, each child with a special need must receive a comprehensive assessment. This assessment guides educators in identification and placement of the child with special needs, as well as in planning appropriate educational programs and interventions.

◆ *Medical diagnosis:* Determination of primary diagnosis by a medical doctor in cases where a medical problem is involved (e.g., visual and hearing impairment, AD/HD, orthopedic and other health impairment)

A person appointed to oversee the assessment process, usually the school psychologist, will be involved in the following procedures:

◆ *Review of cumulative reports and records:* A complete review of all the child's report cards, attendance records, standardized test scores, and so forth, to determine possible patterns of behavior

◆ *Teacher interviews:* Meetings with the classroom teacher to obtain information about the child's basic intellectual, social, and academic performance

◆ *Parent interviews:* Face-to-face meetings with parents to determine essential background history that may be essential for appropriate diagnosis and educational planning

- *Clinical interviews:* Interviews with the child to observe, listen, and make an initial assessment as to where problems may lie

- *Observations:* Watching and recording the child's behavior in the classroom and in other school settings to verify that information from interviews is accurate and to identify any other issues

- *Parent and teacher rating scales:* In the case of the child with AD/HD or other attentional problems, parent and teacher scores on inventories designed to help identify the disorder and assess the child's response to medication

Valuable information is also obtained from testing. Some of these assessments must be administered by the school psychologist. In other cases, a classroom teacher, special educator, speech and language therapist, or occupational therapist will be involved.

- *Sensory functioning assessment:* Tests of hearing and vision, as well as assessment of medical problems: bone, joint, and muscle problems, and health related problems such as allergies, cardiovascular problems, kidney problems, or infectious disesases (e.g., AIDS)

- *Intelligence tests:* Standardized measures of a child's intellectual ability, involving assessment of performance on a number of tasks

- *Achievement tests:* Standardized tests that evaluate a child's academic knowledge by comparing it with an average level of knowledge for the child's grade

- *Perceptual tests:* Measures of the child's abilities to extract information from objects, people, and events in the environment

- *Visual-motor integration tests:* Tests of the child's ability to synchronize visual perceptual input with the use of the hands and fingers

- *Psychological tests:* Measures of a child's affective issues, attitudes and interests, personality, and self-concept

- *Adaptive behavior tests:* Tests of a child's mastery of the many skills required for independent functioning in areas socially prescribed for a given life stage

Students with Multiple Special Needs

While many children with special needs may have only one special need (e.g., visual impairment; chapter 6), some will have multiple special needs, for example, Down syndrome (chapter 9) with severe asthma (chapter 7). Likewise, a child with cerebral palsy (chapter 7) may also be gifted (chapter 11). The situation may be even more complex!

Naturally, having more than one special need presents additional challenges to the child, her family, and you and other school staff. In response, we suggest you study this entire book not only to help the child already identified as having special need(s) but also to alert you to additional needs that that child may display (and that other students may manifest) and prompt your further investigation. Note, too, that many special needs are hidden until a child is older and, for example, is having great difficulty learning to read or showing giftedness in an art form. Often, the most obvious special need can overshadow other special needs, whether they are challenges to overcome or gifts to explore.

Working with Parents

Parents are the child's first and ongoing teachers. Most have their child's best interests at heart as they parent, and parenting is the most difficult job with the least amount of training any of us will ever do. Keep in mind that parents who have a child with a special need have additional stresses, including responding to the child's needs, relating to medical and school staffs, filling out paperwork, making telephone calls to obtain special services, and conducting seemingly endless battles with the health care insurance company. Parents may also suffer from chronic grief and unfounded guilt—the result of their child's suffering—as well as sleep deprivation due to ongoing nighttime care.

It is important to the child's success that you treat his parents with patience, respect, and compassion. You should also try to see the parents as what they are: an invaluable resource for understanding the child's strengths and needs, learning the details of the child's medical and academic history, and providing brainstorming power for troubleshooting classroom issues. Moreover, strive to be a conduit to additional supports (see "Organizations" sections near each chapter's end), a source of affirmation as appropriate, and a trustworthy haven for relief from the otherwise unrelenting stress the care of the child with a special need may cause.

The following two sections list more information for developing positive relationships with the parents of a child with a special need.

General Suggestions

♦ Note that a special need may take vastly differing forms within the range outlined in this book. For example, the child with an anxiety disorder in your class this year may need a completely different approach to succeed in school than the student you had last year with that same disorder. Read further and learn about the specific disorder and its currently recommended treatments and classroom accommodations. Ask the parents to explain the nature of their child's special needs as they understand and have experienced them. Brainstorm a list of strategies that have worked in the past to manage the child's health, academic progress, fears, behavior, and other issues.

- Ask the parents what interests their child. Find ways to incorporate these interests into the child's curriculum and classroom reward system. Doing so can be as simple as, for example, providing books and Web sites on a favorite animal.

- Encourage the parents to list their child's many strengths. This will help you focus on and help develop what the child *can* do. It will also send an encouraging message about the positive approach you plan to take with the child.

- Likewise, ask the parents what their hopes and dreams are for the child. As you plan lessons and communicate with the parents throughout the school year, stay aware and point out how your teaching endeavors may help the child reach her full potential.

- Find out what rewards and teaching methods have been effective in the home. Brainstorm with the parents how these might be adapted for use in the classroom.

- For the child who spends time in a regular classroom, explain the special need to the class, respecting family privacy. Consult the parents and student as to what details may be shared. If possible, allow the child to explain her strengths and needs to her classmates herself. This approach can be very empowering in teaching both the child, by encouraging her to gradually take more responsibility for herself, and the classmates, by helping them focus on the person and her strengths instead of the disability. Parents may also be willing to visit as guest speakers about the special need.

- Connect the parent with school and community organizations and services that may be helpful to the family, such as trained respite care providers (and the funds to pay them), specialized equipment exchanges, assistive technology labs, independent living centers, and parent support groups.

- As needed and appropriate, encourage parents to set up appropriate study space at home and establish consistent routines.

Explain the value of having a structured, set time for homework and academic skills development. Encourage parents to check completed homework.

◆ Since children with, for example, AD/HD, Down syndrome, or emotional disabilities have difficulty understanding different rules for different settings, parents and teachers benefit from working together to develop a consistent set of rules and a similar management system. Respect the parents' beliefs, experiences, and culture.

◆ As with other children, promote the value of reading aloud. This should be a relaxed and fun "quality" time, during which the parents do the "work" and the child enjoys self-selected materials without any pressure to perform (that is, read aloud). Even older children may enjoy this time, especially if the habit is established at a younger age.

◆ In addition, encourage the parent to tape-record one or more chapters in a book so the child can read and look at the words at the same time. This may have the additional positive effect of helping a difficult-to-settle child stay in bed at bedtime. A child with a disability (including a severe emotional or behavioral disability with or without a reading disability) may qualify for the National Library Service for the Blind and Physically Handicapped program through the Library of Congress. Help the parents obtain and fill out the form (which requires a physician's signature) to connect them with this invaluable free service (see "Organizations" section in chapter 6, page 80).

◆ Respect the parents' beliefs, feelings, and decisions regarding medication and other medical decisions.

◆ Likewise, be respectful in regard to the parents' choices of interventions and communication methods if their child has speech, language, or hearing challenges. If possible, encourage the parents to help you learn the child's communication methods and/or to help the class understand the child's communication methods and general strengths.

◆ Be aware that poor behavior or coping skills on the part of the child do not necessarily mean poor parenting skills on the part of the parents. Parents may have developed exceptional parenting skills to nurture their exceptionally challenging child and therefore may resent your implying otherwise. Parents who feel you respect their efforts will be more open to your concerns and ideas.

♦ Work with the parents to reward the child for appropriate behavior, including developing social skills and punctuality. Help parents understand basic positive reinforcement methods.

Effective Parent-Teacher Conferences

Today, there are many effective ways to communicate regularly with parents: newsletters, E-mail, telephone calls, and the like. However, the parent-teacher conference is still a legitimate and valuable tool in promoting effective relationships and encouraging teamwork with parents. The following suggestions will help make your conferences with parents of a child with a special need more effective and profitable:

♦ Hold conferences with parents regularly. This will help reduce tension and miscommunication while providing a reliable format in which parents may express their concerns before they build up. The child will also get the valuable message that you and his parents are working together closely.

♦ Make the parents feel comfortable and relaxed by setting up a pleasant conference environment. Find a quiet, private space; use a table (preferably round) instead of your desk so everyone feels equal; provide adult-sized chairs; and offer refreshments if possible.

♦ Refrain from viewing the parents as adversaries, even if they are angry or hostile. These emotions may be a defense arising from not knowing what your agenda is, years of enduring unpleasant school meetings, and the stress of caring for their child. Since the parents may have legitimate concerns or simply need a chance to "vent," listen without taking anything personally or becoming defensive. Be understanding, patient, and open to suggestions.

♦ One way to reduce parents' anxiety is to be clear before and during the meeting as to the meeting's purpose. Reassure parents that neither you nor other school staff will make any recommendation or change to the child's educational program without their knowledge, input, or permission.

♦ If the purpose of the conference is to explore the possibility of referring the child for testing, explain what you hope to gain from the process. Be solution-oriented and offer realistic hope. Remind the parents that the child may become more resilient and successful at a future stage in development. Let them know their rights to family privacy regarding the process and results.

◆ Provide a pad and pen for parents to take their own notes. After the meeting, give them a copy of your meeting notes to ensure you have communicated clearly. Let them know you welcome their contacting you with any further questions, input, or concerns.

References

American Psychiatric Association (2000). *Diagnostic and Statistical Manual of Mental Disorders* (DSM-IV-TR; 4th ed. rev.). Washington, DC: Author.

Hoy, C., & Gregg, N. (1994). *Assessment: The special educator's role.* Belmont, CA: Brooks/Cole.

CHAPTER 1

Learning Disabilities

Definition

According to the Individuals with Disabilities Education Act (IDEA) a *learning disability* is impairment of one or more of the basic psychological processes involved in understanding or using language, spoken or written, which may manifest itself in an imperfect ability to listen, think, speak, read, write, spell, or calculate mathematical equations. The term encompasses, for example, children with perceptual disabilities, brain injury, and dyslexia. It does not, however, include children who have learning problems that result primarily from visual, hearing, or motor disabilities; developmental disabilities; emotional disabilities; or environmental, cultural, or economic disadvantage. Note, too, that individual states may have varying definitions of learning disabilities. These should be in harmony with federal law.

While having a single term to describe this category of disabilities reduces some confusion, in reality many conflicting theories about the number and causes of learning disabilities exists. The label is all-embracing, describing a syndrome, not a specific child with specific problems. In short, the definition helps classify children, not teach them. Therefore, concentrate on the individual child. Observe both how and how well the child performs: assess strengths and weaknesses and develop ways to help her learn.

In addition, as you study this material, remember that areas of learning interrelate and overlap to a high degree. Thus, a combination of characteristics should not surprise you. Moreover, learning disabilities may mildly, moderately, or severely impair the learning process, depending on the child.

Incidence

A wide range of estimates of the number of children with learning disabilities has appeared in the literature—from 1 to 30 percent of the general population. The U.S. Department of Education (2000) reported that more than 5 percent, or 2.8 million, school-aged children received special education services for learning disabilities.

Characteristics

Learning disabilities are characterized by significant differences in the child's achievement in certain areas, as compared to overall intelligence. Students may exhibit a wide range of specific traits, including deficits in reading comprehension or spoken language, writing, or reasoning ability. Hyperactivity, inattention, and perceptual difficulties may also be associated with learning disabilities. Other possible traits include, for example, unpredictable test performance, perceptual impairments, motor disorders, and challenging behaviors such as impulsiveness, low tolerance of frustration, and difficulty handling day-to-day social interactions.

The following is a list of specific difficulties by area:

- Spoken language: delays, disorders, or discrepancies in listening and speaking

- Written language: difficulties with reading, writing, and spelling

- Arithmetic: difficulty in performing arithmetic functions or comprehending basic concepts

- Reasoning: difficulty in organizing and integrating thoughts

- Organizational skills: difficulty in integrating all facets of learning

- Attention: short span

- Memory: poor letter and/or word memory

- Discrimination: inability to distinguish between letters and their sounds

- Performance: erratic and fluctuating from day to day

- Motor impairment: poor gross and/or fine motor development

- Temporal concepts: difficulty telling time

- Spatial relationships: difficulty visualizing and understanding how objects orient in space

- Mixed dominance: difficulty developing left or right dominance
- Social skills: difficulty making friends
- Behavior: poor and/or inappropriate adjustment to change

Educational Implications

One of the major educational implications for a child with learning disabilities depends on when the disability is first identified. The child has a much better chance of avoiding secondary impairment, for example, emotional tension or loss of self-esteem, if the problem is identified and remedied in the early grades. Further, the secondary behavioral issues may cloud the real issue. For example, avoidance, denial, procrastination, distractibility, and the like are often misunderstood and seen and treated as the "problem," rather than as the result of a learning disability.

Classroom Management Strategies

General Considerations

1. Recognize the student may benefit greatly from the gift of time to grow and mature. Not everyone grows by the clock, especially children with developmental learning issues. Reducing frustration while the child develops should be a primary goal of all educators involved with the student.

2. Provide a high degree of structure, and explain your expectations clearly. The student will tend to have difficulty focusing, getting started, and setting priorities. Creating a clearly structured program exposes the student to fewer distractions, triggering fewer avoidance behaviors and allowing him to focus more on the task at hand.

3. On a related note, provide a regular routine and schedule. Using contracts with the student provides greater structure and helps develop awareness of expectations and personal responsibilities. The student may work best with an hourly, a morning/afternoon, or a daily contract. Take into account the student's learning style, ability levels, motivation, and so on when choosing a contract type.

4. Make sure needed learning materials are easily accessible, well-organized, and stored in the same place each day. The less the student has to worry about, comprehend, or remember, the better. Too many details can easily overwhelm the student.

5. Whenever possible, use self-correcting materials, providing immediate feedback without embarrassing the student.

6. Give assignments (including homework assignments) in an easy, clear, and accessible manner. Writing the assignments down for the child in a notebook or on a chalkboard and also presenting them orally are helpful. Then go over the list and details to find and dispel areas of confusion. This reduces frustration for the student, parents, and you. Consider tape-recording the assignments. Appealing to more than one sense helps the child comprehend assignment expectations accurately. Do not assume anything. Not all students with learning disabilities will need this one-on-one support, but those who do should receive it.

7. Break down long assignments involving several steps into smaller parts. For long-term assignments, recognize that the parts are greater than the whole when it comes to increasing chances of completion and learning. If a project has several steps, explain the general principal and goal with the child, then help her focus on one part at a time. Guide her to each subsequent step only *after* she has completed the previous step.

8. Making shorter but more frequent assignments also takes a child's feelings of control and accomplishment into consideration. Many children feel out of control because they are frequently unable to finish assignments or get high grades. Using shorter but more frequent assignments also allows you to monitor the student's progress more closely throughout the assignment, helping you to recognize any difficulties before the child wastes precious time and patience doing a long assignment inaccurately.

9. Shorten the overall length of the assignments to help ensure a sense of success and self-worth, which, as we cannot emphasize enough, is more important than anything to learning.

10. Create structure as explained in the first several tips, but at the same time also allow flexibility in classroom procedures (e.g., using tape recorders for note and test taking when the student has trouble writing). Keep in mind that the greater the number of options in responding to a task, the greater chance the student's learning style(s) will be useful and therefore successful.

11. Testing should also be flexible, allowing for untimed or oral responses. Even if the IEP does not list such accommodation, try alternate forms of responses to see which one works best for the child to improve performance and therefore self-confidence.

12. Maintain constant communication among special education teacher, regular classroom teacher, teaching assistants, and any other teachers and tutors. Nothing confuses a child with learning disabilities more than several adults' each taking different approaches and telling him differing ways to handle skills or situations. The student will have the best chance to improve only if the help is well-coordinated and noncontradictory.

13. Likewise, maintain constant communication with parents (e.g., through handwritten notes, E-mail, progress reports, and/or phone communication). Breaking down fears, misconceptions, and assumptions is crucial to the child's success. The more you and the parents work as a team, the greater the chance the educational plan will work.

14. Be aware the student may have problems processing information, slowing both verbal and written responses. Allow the student time to respond that is sufficient for *her*.

15. Whenever possible, be flexible with grading. For example, avoid handing back failing work with an actual grade marked. Write "See me" on it, then allow the child to redo the assignment, especially if the child made an effort to succeed. Remember, many factors make tests and assignments difficult for children with learning disabilities—none of these factors is "on purpose." Having the chance to redo an assignment with appropriate supports can and does help build a feeling of success within the child. The child, however, may lack resiliency, either because he has failed too often or as part of the disability itself. Thus, he may become defensive on seeing he did not do well. If this response becomes a pattern, then reexamine your expectations and/or the nature of your assignments, redesigning them to increase the student's chances for learning—and success.

16. Star correct problems first, providing a foundation of success and positive feedback. Then say, in reference to the incorrect problems, something such as, "I bet if you do this one over, you may get a different answer; give it a try."

17. Address problems with organization by making sure the child's desk stays cleared of all unnecessary materials. The less chaos, the better the focus. Specifically, have the child use small binders that hold fewer papers. Have the child bring in a small trash can to place right next to his desk so he can immediately throw out papers he doesn't need to keep. Otherwise, he may be embarrassed to get up to go to the trash can and instead stuff the papers in his desk.

18. Whenever the child hands in work, she may begin to worry about how she did. If she has to wait too long for feedback, she may needlessly waste a great deal of energy worrying. Correct the student's work as soon as possible so you can prevent such a reaction.

19. Provide several alternatives in both obtaining and reporting information: tapes, interviews, and so on. The greater the number of alternate response methods, the greater the chance for success.

20. Permit the child to work in a quiet corner, such as a study carrel, when requested or necessary. Don't place the child there all the time because isolation may have negative consequences, but stay tuned into the specific learning style and needs of the child.

21. At first, consider placing the child closer to you for more immediate feedback. Proximity to you also offers the child a sense of structure and a greater chance for personal attention.

22. At the same time, try to separate the student from peers who may be distracting. The child may simply be very distractible or may have learned to use any external situation to avoid potential failure. Seating the child next to students who are self-motivated and internally controlled will provide positive peer models, helping the child develop self-control.

23. Alternate quiet and active time to maintain high levels of interest and motivation. Allow the child rest periods between work periods. The child may fatigue in academic tasks more easily than other children.

24. Keep work periods short, gradually lengthening them as the student begins to cope better. Do not increase work periods too quickly, however; focus instead on first building a firm foundation of success.

25. Encourage the student to write notes and memos to herself, listing important words, concepts, and ideas. Tape a small notebook to the desk to facilitate this process. At the end of the day, have her rip out the page and take it home or throw it out if it is no longer needed.

26. Type all handouts: The student may find typed work easier to read and comprehend. Do not assume the child can read your handwriting.

27. Be aware of the conditions that may trigger the child's frustrations. He may have a frustration "aura" that occurs before cer-

tain behaviors. Learn to recognize a sign such as this as well as the types of situations that may lead to such overreactions or frustration.

Academic Considerations

28. Give the student large graph paper to use when doing computing. Placing one number in each box will allow the child to maintain neat and, most important, correct columns.

29. Allow the student to do only three to five math problems at a time to help him focus on accuracy. Along the same lines, limit each new assignment practice sheet to five to ten easy problems total to further build a foundation of success, fostering openness and resiliency in learning.

30. Allow the student to repeat word problems in her own words while identifying the critical parts of the problem.

31. Use real-world situations for word problems. Personalizing word problems heightens motivation and focus. In short, make the problems as close to the child's real life as possible.

32. Enlarge the computation signs (e.g., +, −, =) to reduce the likelihood of the child's mixing up signs that may look alike to him.

33. Whenever possible, provide math tables. While there is no doubt that having the math facts memorized enhances speed and accuracy, the reality is that some children may never be able to memorize. So give them math tables, reducing frustration and tension, keeping feelings of success and accomplishment as the primary goals. In the same vein, we strongly suggest you allow the student to use a calculator.

34. To further develop feelings of accomplishment and success, always design math problem sheets with problems in ascending order of difficulty.

35. Whenever possible, use manipulative objects to demonstrate and illustrate math concepts. Objects tend to crystallize certain abstract concepts for all children but especially for the child with a learning disability.

36. For a child with visual-motor difficulties, create spelling tests for which the child has to circle the correctly spelled word out of four choices. This will reduce the need for motor input that may be the true reason for low grades on written spelling tests. In addition, make sure the spelling tests cover no more than five words at a time.

37. As an alternative, have the child grade five to ten of his peers' spelling tests. He will have to learn the word in order to correct it but will not have to face the possibility of failing the test, especially if spelling is a severe challenge for him. Double-check the child's correcting privately.

38. Have the child read the questions to a chapter before reading it to help her know what she is to look for as she reads. The child may try to memorize everything if she is not sure what will be asked—most likely an impossible tactic for the child with a learning disability.

39. Make photocopies of text the child has to read so she can use a highlighter pen to underline important facts. Not only will this help her focus better, it will also provide practice for and reinforcement of a variety of study skills (e.g., making notes in the margins, circling key words, and the like).

40. To reinforce capitalization rules, have the child use a marker to highlight the first letter in each new sentence.

41. Provide high-interest, low-vocabulary reading materials. For example, for reading comprehension fun, ask the child to write a review of a comic book he is currently enjoying reading.

42. Have the student make her own personal dictionary consisting of all the spelling words she learns. Continue this activity on an ongoing basis, pointing out how much she has accomplished as the dictionary lengthens throughout the year.

43. If a child has serious writing challenges, allow another student to make a copy of his notes or use carbon paper so you can direct the child to focus only on the lecture. Or give him a copy of your notes. Doing so may enhance listening skills.

44. Offer many different types of writing assignments: creative, expository, narrative, process, and so on.

45. Provide line markers for the student who loses her place while reading. Use index cards, rulers, and the like. Show her how to use the marker to keep her place.

46. Give the child a disposable camera with which to take pictures she may later create a written story about. The motivation for writing is always greater when the subject is part of everyday life—not to mention children generally find using a camera fun.

47. Motivate the student by providing him with an interesting short story, long joke, anecdote, or the like that includes a number of

spelling mistakes. Direct the child to try to circle all the mistakes in the passage.

48. Review rules for capitalization and punctuation *before* the student begins writing.

49. Teach writing as a three-step process: prewriting, writing, and rewriting. Explain that having to rewrite is a natural part of the process for all writers—not a sign of failure.

50. Match the student with a peer helper to assist with understanding assignments, reading important directions, drilling the student orally, summarizing important textbook passages, and working on long-term assignments.

51. Use computers with age- and ability-appropriate software for drill and practice and teaching word processing.

52. If possible, use raised-line paper for a child with writing control problems. Otherwise, use a straightedge to go over lines with a black marker. Doing so will help the student with visual-motor challenges maintain better line control.

Perceptual Considerations

53. Use short sentences and a simple vocabulary. The child may have problems with both short-term memory and processing information quickly. The child may not comprehend or may simply forget lengthy directions, messages, requests, and so on. "No-frills" directions and other communication may help reduce or prevent frustration.

54. Whenever possible, use multisensory teaching methods. This is both a commonsense and a research-supported tactic. The more senses a student uses to learn a concept, fact, or skill, the more likely the student will understand and retain the information. Use a combination of visual, auditory, kinesthetic, and tactile input.

55. As mentioned earlier, give the student oral rather than written tests. This may be especially helpful for children with serious writing problems or other visual-motor deficits.

56. Help the student learn to drill herself on important information—for example, by reciting information into a tape recorder and playing it back or having the student drill aloud to herself or another student. Auditory feedback for the child who is an auditory learner is crucial.

57. Have the child close her eyes to try to listen better to words or information. She should also practice visualizing words and information in her mind. Share some ideas for how she might "see" something.

58. Offer flash cards printed in bold, bright colors.

59. When selecting or developing worksheets, include only a few questions or problems per page. This will help prevent the child from becoming confused, overwhelmed, and/or intimidated by too much visual stimuli.

Social Skills Development

60. Provide positive reinforcement for use of appropriate social skills at school. Make sure parents understand the concept of positive reinforcement so they may reinforce school-based strategies at home. Give lots of practical suggestions; many parents believe that positive reinforcement only means buying something at a toy store. Explain your suggestions to both the parents and the child.

61. Clearly define the specific social behaviors you feel are a priority. During a calm time, privately discuss with the child alternative behaviors that would result in more positive feelings and successful outcomes. When a child has ongoing social skills acquisition challenges, ensure the IEP defines social skill goals and teaching methods.

62. Select a student to be the child's "social coach" to help him master appropriate social skills.

Student-Teacher Interaction

63. Know and capitalize on the student's strengths, building on these through repeated successful experiences. Feelings of accomplishment and success help balance out the frustration the student experiences with academic tasks.

64. To further foster self-esteem, create a supportive teaching-learning atmosphere in which each child may be successful.

65. Show a special interest in the child, letting him know that you value his work. Being recognized is a basic human need, especially when one is trying one's best to accomplish something. "Best," however, is a relative term for the child with a learning disability; find aspects of the child's work you can recognize as a positive accomplishment.

66. Respond to and praise the child's communication efforts whenever possible. The child may have emotional issues arising from the frustration and lower sense of self-worth created by academic stress and failure. It is essential to affirm him when he takes the risk of communicating (e.g., through participating in discussions and initiating conversations).

67. Hold the student accountable for what she is capable of doing. Two of the biggest mistakes possible are making excuses and rationalizing away poor performance or effort for the student. Do not do the student a disservice by lowering your expectations based on fears of the student's failing or experiencing frustration. Such an approach may create "learned helplessness" in a child who is capable of much more than you may recognize. Get a good idea of a child's abilities and skill levels, then hold her accountable—a real-world lesson for a lifetime of success!

68. Give continual feedback. The child may have already memorized negative "scripts" about her abilities and performances. Feedback in any form reduces this negative energy pattern and offers reality, the only thing that breaks down fear.

69. Hold frequent (even if short) conferences with the child to answer his questions, find his sources of confusion, reduce avoidance behaviors, monitor appropriateness of class work, and increase his sense of connection to you and the educational setting.

70. Teach the child how to set realistic goals. A history of failure and the need for immediate success may make this difficult for her. She may believe, for example, she must get "100" on the next test or do a task perfectly to get back the recognition or feelings of self-worth she has lost. But when this does not occur, she may falter even more.

71. As mentioned earlier, limit the number of choices the child has to make every day. Structure, routine, and guidance build trust, offering the child a pathway to hope and success.

Organizations

Council for Learning Disabilities (CLD)
P.O. Box 40303
Overland Park, KS 66204
913–492–8755
Web site: www.cldinternational.org

Division of Learning Disabilities
Council for Exceptional Children
1920 Association Drive
Reston, VA 22091–1589
703–620–3660
888–CEC–SPED (888–232–7733; toll-free)
TTY: 703–264–9446
Web site: www.cec.sped.org
E-mail: service@cec.sped.org

International Dyslexia Association
    (formerly the "Orton Dyslexia Society")
Chester Building, Suite 382
8600 LaSalle Road
Baltimore, MD 21286–2044
410–296–0232
800–222–3123
Web site: www.interdys.org
E-mail: info@interdys.org

Learning Disabilities Association of America (LDA)
4156 Library Road
Pittsburgh, PA 15234–1349
412–341–1515
888–300–6710 (toll-free)
Web site: www.ldanatl.org
E-mail: ldanatl@usaor.net

National Center for Learning Disabilities
381 Park Avenue South, Suite 1401
New York, NY 10016
212–545–7510
888–575–7373 (toll-free)
Web site: www.ncld.org

References and Bibliography

Balter, A. (1996). *Coping with learning disabilities: A book for parents.* Dubuque, IA: Kendall-Hunt.

Fornes, S. R., & Kaball, K. A. (1995). *The nature of learning disabilities.* Hillsdale, NJ: Erlbaum.

Hall, D. E. (1993). *Living with learning disabilities: A guide for students.* Minneapolis: Lerner.

Hallowell, E. M., & Ratey, J. J. (1996). *Answers to distractions.* New York: Bantam.

Henley, M., Ramsey, R. S., & Algozzine, R. (1999). *Characteristics of and strategies for teaching students with mild disabilities.* Needham Heights, MA: Allyn & Bacon.

Journal of Learning Disabilities. Available from PRO-ED, 8700 Shoal Creek Boulevard, Austin, TX 78758; 512–451–3246.

Lab School of Washington. (1993). *Issues of parenting children with learning disabilities* (audiotapes). Washington, DC: Author.

Lerner, J. (1997). *Learning disabilities: Theories, diagnoses and teaching strategies.* Boston: Houghton Mifflin.

Olivier, C., & Bowler, R. F. (1996). *Learning to learn.* New York: Fireside.

Rourke, B. P. (1999). *Nonverbal learning disabilities: The syndrome and the model.* New York: Guilford.

Silver, L. (1991). *The misunderstood child: A guide for parents of children with learning disabilities* (2nd ed.). New York: McGraw-Hill.

Smith, C., & Strick, L. (1997). *Learning disabilities A to Z: A parent's complete guide to learning disabilities from preschool to adulthood.* New York: Free Press.

Smith, S. (1995). *No easy answers* (rev. ed.). New York: Bantam.

Smith, T. E., Dowdy, C. A., Polloway, E. A., & Blalock, G. (1996). *Children and adults with learning disabilities.* Needham Heights, MA: Allyn and Bacon.

Tuttle, C., & Paquette, P. (1993). *Parenting a child with a learning disability.* Los Angeles: Lowell House.

U.S. Department of Education. (2000). *Twenty-second annual report to Congress on the implementation of the Individuals with Disabilities Education Act.* Washington, DC: Author.

Wong, B. (1996). *The ABCs of learning disabilities.* San Diego: Academic.

Wong, L. Y. (1998). *Learning about learning disabilities.* San Diego: Academic.

CHAPTER 2

Attention-Deficit/ Hyperactivity Disorder

Definition

Attention-Deficit/Hyperactivity Disorder (AD/HD) is a neurobiological disorder. Typically, children with AD/HD have developmentally inappropriate behavior, including poor attention skills and, often, high impulsivity and activity. These characteristics arise in early childhood, typically before age 7; are chronic; and persist for at least 6 months. Children with AD/HD may also experience problems in the areas of social skills and self-esteem.

Although most laypeople, and even some professionals, still call it ADD (the name given in 1980), the diagnostic name is officially Attention-Deficit/Hyperactivity Disorder, or AD/HD. This change in name is the result of scientific advances and reflects the findings of careful field trials; researchers now have strong evidence to support the position that AD/HD is one specific disorder with different variations. Currently, researchers divide AD/HD into three subtypes:

AD/HD, Predominantly Inattentive Type

AD/HD, Predominantly Hyperactive-Impulsive Type

AD/HD, Combined Type

The subtypes are divided according to the main features associated with the disorder: inattentiveness, impulsivity, and hyperactivity. Some children with AD/HD have little or no trouble sitting still or inhibiting interfering behavior but may be predominantly inattentive. These children, diagnosed as having AD/HD of the predominantly inattentive type, have great difficulty getting or staying focused on a task. Other children with AD/HD may be able to pay attention to a task but lose focus because they have trouble controlling their impulses and activity levels. They are properly diagnosed as having AD/HD of predominantly hyperactive-impulsive type. The most prevalent subtype, however, is the combined type. Children with this diagnosis will have significant symptoms of all three main characteristics.

Incidence

AD/HD is estimated to affect 3 to 7 percent of the school-aged population. Even though the exact cause of AD/HD remains unknown, it is known that AD/HD is a neurobiologically based disorder. Research also suggests that AD/HD is genetically transmitted and that the disorder may result from a chemical imbalance or deficiency in the brain—specifically, abnormalities in the dopamine system.

Characteristics

From time to time all children will be inattentive, impulsive, and overly active. In the case of AD/HD, however, these behaviors are the rule, not the exception. AD/HD is diagnosed according to certain characteristics: A child with AD/HD is often described as having a short attention span and as being distractible. The child has difficulty with one or all parts of the attention process:

- Focusing—picking something to pay attention to
- Sustaining focus—paying attention for as long as is needed
- Shifting focus—moving attention from one thing to another

  Some frequently seen symptoms of inattention include the following:

- Fails to pay close attention to details, making careless mistakes in schoolwork or other activities
- Difficulty maintaining attention in tasks or play activities
- Appears not to be listening when spoken to directly
- Difficulty following through on instructions, for example, may fail to finish schoolwork, chores, or duties (not due to oppositional behavior or not understanding instructions)
- Trouble organizing tasks and activities

- Avoids, dislikes, or is reluctant to engage in tasks that require sustained mental effort (e.g., schoolwork and homework)

- Loses things necessary for tasks or activities (e.g., toys, school assignments, pencils, books, or tools)

- Easily distracted by extraneous stimuli

- Forgetful in daily activities

Some frequently seen symptoms of hyperactivity include the following:

- Fidgets with hands or feet or squirms in seat

- Leaves seat in classroom and other situations in which staying seated is expected

- Runs about or climbs excessively in inappropriate situations

- Difficulty playing or engaging in leisure activities quietly

- Seems "on the go" or acts as if "driven by a motor"

- Talks excessively

"Acting before thinking" is a good way to describe impulsiveness with children with AD/HD. Some frequently seen symptoms of impulsivity include the following:

- Blurts out answers before questions have been completed

- Difficulty awaiting turn

- Interrupts or intrudes on others (e.g., during conversations or games)

Educational Implications

Many children with AD/HD experience great difficulty in school, where attention and impulse and motor control are clearly requirements for success. A child with AD/HD tends to overreact to changes in the environment. Indeed, whether at home or school, the child will likely respond best within a structured, predictable environment. Therefore, make rules and expectations clear and consistent. Then outline clear consequences ahead of time and deliver these immediately as needed. Structure and routines cultivate an environment that encourages the child to control her behavior while helping her learn.

Classroom Management Strategies

General Considerations

1. Whenever possible, avoid steps with more than one instruction and multipart assignments. Allow the child to finish one assignment or direction at a time before offering him the next.

2. Designate a specific place where the child should place completed assignments.

3. If the child is capable at this stage, teach her to keep a daily homework journal. Or prepare a copy of the homework assignments to give to the child at the end of the day. This will alleviate a great deal of stress on the part of the child by creating a more comfortable and successful environment, especially if she is disorganized and frequently forgets to list the assignments for herself. Having the child do the homework is more important than learning to remember to copy the assignment.

4. Give shorter but more frequent assignments to increase success rates. Break long-term projects into short-term assignments. Reward the child for completing each step. Remember, confidence builds through repeated successful experiences.

5. Ask parents to help the child get organized each night before school. Encourage them to develop a checklist so the child's clothes, books, assignments, and so on are ready for the next morning. Explain that stress and disorganization in the morning should be avoided at all costs so the child arrives at school feeling calm and secure rather than "rattled."

6. At the other end of the school day, provide enough time for the child to get his materials together to take home.

7. If necessary, have the child finish all assignments in school. At times, the child may be so inattentive that sending homework home to be accomplished may result in more stress, especially in interactions with parents (who, keep in mind, have enough to deal with already and need to be able to foster a positive relationship with the child to increase self-esteem and therefore learning). Higher stress may make the child even more agitated, creating a vicious cycle.

8. A child with organizational problems will usually take very disorganized notes and have a messy notebook, desk, and locker. Create time for and help the child learn to organize these areas weekly. For example, require the child to clean out her desk each

day so that papers are kept in order. Making this area part of the general class routine will also help her feel better about herself.

9. Use boxes, bins, or other organizers to help the child separate and store various items.

10. Encourage the use of binders or individual folders to help keep schoolwork organized. Set up a special place for tools, materials, and books. Organization and routine are critical to success.

11. If possible, do not place the student near distracting stimuli, such as an air conditioner, heater, high traffic areas, doors, or windows. Create a "stimuli-reduced" study area. Let all students be allowed to go to this area so that the student with AD/HD will not feel self-conscious or singled out.

12. Likewise, make sure any work space is clean. Clutter and disorganization can be very disruptive to the child's learning process. Direct her to put away anything she doesn't need at the moment.

13. Avoid planning numerous transitions and changes throughout the day. Clearly list and explain the daily schedule to help the child deal with change.

14. Be flexible with classroom procedures, and plan many breaks throughout the day.

15. Although the child will likely be easily distracted, simple methods can help her focus her attention, including placing her near your desk or in the front row; maintaining eye contact with her; using gestures to emphasize points; and providing a work area away from distractions. Stand near the student while lecturing. This is called "proximity control."

16. Try to preempt the child's behavior, especially during changes in the schedule. Inform the child of the change about 5 minutes beforehand and define your expectations for appropriate behavior.

17. As appropriate to the age and situation, identify strengths in the child you can publicly announce or praise. This will help the other students develop a more positive perception of the child. For example, a kindergartner will love it when you show the class his stunning artwork, but a teen may feel more open to affirmation through your facilitating (with his permission) his having his photographs published in the local or school newspaper.

18. Instead of risking the detrimental effects of placing the child in large groups, initially expose the child to small group interactions. Placing a child with AD/HD in large groups may be detrimental. Help the group set goals and create interdependency so they can accomplish some simple task successfully. To implement this, use study carrels, run small groups at the back of the classroom, and so forth.

19. If the child has problems listening and taking notes, have a peer "buddy" take notes while using carbon paper. This reduces the stress of listening and writing simultaneously. Or give the child a copy of your notes.

20. If the child takes any medication (e.g., Ritalin), protect her privacy (e.g., by avoiding publicly reminding her to go down to the nurse's office to take it).

21. Reinforce word processing, typing, spell checking, and other computer skills. The computer can be very motivating, and the end product (e.g., a typed report) will make the child feel very good about herself.

22. Create chances for peer interaction and cooperative learning for academic tasks that do not require sitting for long periods of time.

Academic Considerations

23. Allow extra time for taking tests and completing assignments, including homework, whether or not these accommodations are listed in the child's IEP. Do not be arbitrary; instead, reflect the "real" time required by the child. See if the child's performance improves.

24. Permit other forms of reporting information (e.g., audiotapes, role-playing, simulations, videotapes, and two- and three-dimensional artwork).

25. Give the child large-squared graph paper on which to do math, providing the structure needed to keep numbers lined up correctly. Generally, the larger the squares, the easier it will be for the child to place one number in each box. Doing this will also help him stay focused.

26. Allow the student to use a calculator or basic math tables when doing assignments. Setting him up for success is the key here. If the child becomes frustrated because he can't recall the facts, he may give up altogether.

27. Single out math problems so the child sees only one at a time. For example, create a "window" by cutting out a paper "frame" the child may move from one problem to the next. Make the frame large enough to cover all or most of the other problems while the child works on the one in the window.

28. Give the older child a printed sheet of science or math formulas needed. Asking the child to memorize may reduce her ability to actually accomplish the task. The less she has to worry about, the more she may be able to finish.

29. Carefully design academic tasks to be manageable and clear.

30. Specifically, determine what your goal is when presenting an assignment. This "paves all the roads" for the child up to that point. For example, if your goal is to see if the child can find the circumference of a circle, provide him with the formulas, definitions, and examples. Such an approach will reduce frustration and confusion, increasing chances of success.

31. Do not use "bubble" answer sheets. Allow the child to answer directly in the booklet or on the paper. Reducing the amount of physical movement during academic tasks is more beneficial because it is likely the child has difficulty refocusing.

32. Encourage peer tutoring and cooperative and collaborative learning.

33. Frequently remind the student about assignments that are due so he doesn't lose academic credit for not completing or turning in work. Set clear deadlines and consistently remind the student of the deadline. Then periodically check the notebook and any other materials to make sure the child is staying organized, keeping pace with classmates, and following directions.

34. Direct the child to do only five problems, two questions, or the like at a time. Then have her come to you for immediate feedback. Numerous successful tasks add to her self-confidence. This will also prevent the child from progressing too far while making the same error.

35. Seat the child next to a student who is very focused. This peer model will help the child focus.

36. Have the parents sign a daily notebook you send home, informing them of the work that still needs to be completed.

37. Build self-confidence by starting each assignment with a few questions or activities you know the student can successfully answer or accomplish.

38. Intensify instruction by repeating main points several times.

39. Providing more stimulation and variety in a controlled manner may improve the performance and behavior of the student with AD/HD. You can alter the assignment (e.g., "Make up a song instead of writing your ideas"), the activity (e.g., "Show me a thunderstorm with your body instead of explaining it in words"), or even the color of the paper used.

40. Send all homework assignments home with clear instructions for the parents.

41. When you ask a student with AD/HD a question, begin the question with the child's name and then pause for a few seconds to signal the child to pay close attention.

42. Simplify complex verbal directions. Avoid multiple commands. Note, too, that the child may need both verbal and visual directions.

43. The child may need more help than peers in learning strategies to help him study and organize his work more efficiently. Develop listening skills, outline routines, structure tasks, and help the child organize his notebook(s). Teach all students techniques for taking notes from both lectures and textbooks. It may also be helpful to give the student an outline for taking his own notes, listing the main concepts in advance.

44. Use interactive CD-ROM reading programs. The multisensory stimulation will help keep the child focused. However, make sure the program does not require the child to do too many tasks at one time, possibly overloading her.

45. Use books on tape, borrowed from the school or city library, so the child can read and listen at the same time.

46. Use manipulative/hands-on materials as much as possible.

47. Develop mnemonic devices to aid in memory skills. For example, help the class or student think up silly rhymes to remember science concepts.

48. Give the child a tape recorder to help him drill himself.

49. When appropriate, have the class read in unison instead of having the child read aloud solo. This helps all students focus and learn.

50. At other times, you alone could read along with the child, adding valuable sensory feedback and pacing to help the child stay more focused.

Psychological Considerations

51. Learn to recognize and understand the child's frustration triggers. Knowing that a child with AD/HD is about to lose focus may help you prevent inappropriate behavior and feelings of failure.

52. Encourage positive thinking (e.g., "You did a great job staying on task. How do you feel about your day?"). This, along with successful experiences, can improve self-esteem and therefore learning.

53. Teach the child an "emotional vocabulary" so he can release his stress with words instead of aggressive behavior. Having the appropriate words enhances the child's ability to express his feelings.

54. When the child has an adequate emotional vocabulary, begin to work on teaching him to verbalize his anger and other strong emotions in a healthy manner. Explain to him that it is OK to be upset but that he must learn how to express his feelings in a socially acceptable manner. Explain that many times it is how he says something that creates problems, not the emotion itself.

55. Keep in mind that the child may feel out of control and helpless. This feeling can lead to depression and victimization. Try to empower the child by focusing on all the parts of her life over which she does have control. Regularly affirm her strengths.

Behavior Management

56. Always stay calm, positive, and upbeat to show you are in control of the situation.

57. An effective management system concentrates on a few behaviors at a time, with new behavior patterns added when the student masters the first ones. Reinforce appropriate behavior with something the student is willing to work for (or to avoid). For example, give or remove points immediately, according to the behavior, so the child understands why he is or is not being rewarded. While older children may be willing to work toward a deferred reward, younger children generally need more immediate reinforcement.

58. If you use a reward system with a younger child, you may want to make charts or tokens or stickers to show her the consequences and positive results of her behavior. Be honest, however, with yourself in respect to the reward system you have established. If it is not effective, be flexible enough to change it.

59. An important aspect of time-out, an effective consequence for inappropriate behavior, is removing the privilege of choosing where the child would like to be or how time is spent. In general, the child stays in time-out and must be quiet for 5 minutes. Preschool-aged children are usually given 2 or 3 minutes in time-out. For toddlers, 30 seconds to a minute is appropriate. A time-out should never be longer than 1 minute per age of the child (e.g., 8 minutes for an 8-year-old).

60. Another proven strategy is to provide a specified "positive time-out" location to which the student can go when he recognizes he is not in control. This should not be presented or seen as a punishment but as a place for the student to go for a few minutes to calm down. Systematically, teach older students to sense when they are getting out of control and go to the time-out area on their own.

61. We cannot emphasize enough that you must be extremely consistent in enforcing classroom rules so the child knows you are serious about your procedures and policies. Set few but firm rules and limits, then be sure to enforce the ones you have—immediately!

62. Be realistic, however, about your expectations for the child's behavior. Choose your guidelines and "battles" wisely. Ignore minor incidents and focus on the more intrusive or inappropriate ones.

63. Build in periods of time when it is OK for the child to leave her seat for some activity (e.g., collecting homework, getting materials for you from the closet, and so on).

64. As mentioned earlier, you can help the student shift from one task to another by providing clear and consistent transitions between activities or alerting him a few minutes before changing activities.

65. Place the student with her back to the class to keep other students out of view.

66. Frequently praise the child for staying on task. This gives the child the feedback necessary to understand the specifics of his own positive behavior.

Social Skills Development

67. Assign a monitoring peer "buddy" to offer the child feedback and hints about appropriate and inappropriate behaviors. This

may be especially helpful during more chaotic and noisy times (e.g., recess and lunch).

68. Role-play social situations with the child, emphasizing using specific skills. This will help the child develop a "toolbox" of social skills he can practice applying in everyday situations.

69. Work one on one with the child to set up a social contract clearly outlining the goals he would like to accomplish. Mutually agree on only one goal at a time to help him focus and be more successful. Also point out and include the behaviors that may be required to attain these goals.

Medication Considerations

70. Medication has proven effective for many children with AD/HD. Most experts agree, however, that medication should never be the only treatment used. The parents' decision to place a child on medication is a personal one and should be made after a thorough evaluation of the child has taken place and after careful consideration by both the parents and the physician.

71. Stimulants are the medication most widely prescribed for AD/HD. These drugs (e.g., Ritalin [the most widely used], Dexedrine, Cylert) are believed to stimulate the brain's neurotransmitters, enabling the brain to better regulate attention, impulse, and motor behavior. In general, the short-acting stimulant medications (e.g., Ritalin, Dexedrine) have few and mild side effects. For children who cannot take stimulant drugs, a physician may prescribe antidepressants or clonidine (a blood pressure medication that has a sedative effect on many children with AD/HD).

72. The prescribing physician should explain the benefits and drawbacks of medication to the parents and, when appropriate, to the child. Doses are generally increased gradually so the child receives the lowest dose needed to achieve the greatest therapeutic benefit. Parents should dispense the medication as prescribed and monitor closely how their child responds, including side effects. Such monitoring generally includes feedback from the child's teacher(s), which is usually obtained from behavior rating scales. Parents then communicate with the physician as often as necessary to determine when medication has reached the proper level for the child and to discuss any problems or concerns.

Organizations

CHADD (Children and Adults
    with Attention Deficit/Hyperactivity Disorder)
8181 Professional Place, Suite 201
Landover, MD 20785
301–306–7070
800–233–4050
Web site: www.chadd.org

National Attention Deficit Disorder Association (ADDA)
1788 Second Street, Suite 200
Highland Park, IL 60035
847–432–ADDA (847–432–2332)
800–487–2282
Web site: www.add.org
E-mail: mail@add.org

References and Bibliography

Alexander-Roberts, C. (1994). *ADHD parenting handbook: Practical advice for parents from parents—Proven techniques for raising a hyperactive child without losing your temper.* Dallas: Taylor.

Barkley, R. A. (1990). *Attention deficit with hyperactivity disorder: A handbook for diagnosis and treatment.* New York: Guilford.

Barkley, R. A. (1995). *Taking charge of ADHD: The complete authoritative guide for parents.* New York: Guilford.

Coleman, W. S. (1993). *Attention deficit with hyperactivity disorder: A handbook for parents and professionals.* Madison, WI: Calliope.

Dendy, S. A. Z. (1995). *Teenagers with ADD: A parent's guide.* Bethesda: Woodbine.

Dowdy, C. (1998). *Attention deficit disorder in the classroom: A practical guide for teachers.* Austin: PRO-ED.

DuPaul, G. J., & Stoner, G. (1994). *ADHD in the schools: Assessment and intervention strategies.* New York: Guilford.

Fowler, M. (1992). *CHADD educators' manual: An in-depth look at attention deficit disorders from an educational perspective.* Landover, MD: Children and Adults with Attention Deficit/Hyperactivity Disorder.

Fowler, M. (1994). *Attention-deficit/hyperactivity disorder* (Briefing Paper 1–16). Washington, DC: National Information Center for Children and Youth with Disabilities.

Fowler, M. (1996). *Maybe you know my kid: A parent's guide to identifying, understanding, and helping your child with ADHD* (3rd ed.). New York: Birch Lane.

Goldstein, S. (1990). *Managing attention deficit disorders in children.* New York: Wiley.

Goldstein, S., & Goldstein, M. (1992). *Hyperactivity: Why won't my child pay attention? A complete guide to ADD for parents, teachers, and community agencies.* New York: Wiley.

Gordon, M. (1990). *ADHD: A consumer's guide*. DeWitt, NY: GSI.

Hallowell, M. E., & Ratey, J. J. (1996). *Answers to distractions*. New York: Bantam.

Hanley, J. L. (1999). *Attention deficit disorder*. Green Bay: IMPAKT.

Latham, P. S., & Latham, P. H. (1992). *Attention deficit disorder and the law: A guide for advocates*. Washington, DC: JKL Communications.

Lerner, J. (1995). *Attention deficit disorder*. New York: Brooks-Cole.

Lynn, G. T. (1996). *Survival strategies for parenting your ADD child*. Grass Valley, CA: Underwood.

Rief, S. (1993). *How to reach and teach ADD children*. West Nyack, NY: Simon & Schuster.

Robin, A. L., & Barkley, R. A. (1998). *ADHD in adolescents: Diagnosis and treatment*. New York: Guilford.

Silver, L. B. (1992). *Attention deficit hyperactivity disorder: A clinical guide to diagnosis and treatment*. Washington, DC: American Psychiatric Press.

Taylor, J. F. (1994). *Helping your ADHD child*. New York: Werner.

U. S. Department of Education. (1991). *Clarification of policy to address the needs of children with attention deficit disorders within general and/or special education*. Washington, DC: Author.

Weingartner, P. L. (1999). *ADHD handbook for families: A guide to communicating with professionals*. Washington, DC: Child Welfare League of America.

Wodrich, D. L. (1994). *Attention deficit hyperactivity disorder: What every parent wants to know*. Baltimore: P. H. Brookes.

CHAPTER 3

Emotional Disabilities

Definition

Many terms are used to describe emotional, behavioral, or mental disorders. Currently, students with such disorders may be categorized as having a serious emotional disturbance, which is defined under the IDEA as follows:

> A condition exhibiting one or more of the following characteristics over a long time and to a marked degree that adversely affects educational performance—
>
> (A) An inability to learn that cannot be explained by intellectual, sensory, or health factors;
>
> (B) An inability to build or maintain satisfactory interpersonal relationships with peers and teachers;
>
> (C) Inappropriate types of behavior or feelings under normal circumstances;
>
> (D) A general pervasive mood of unhappiness or depression; or
>
> (E) A tendency to develop physical symptoms or fears associated with personal or school problems.

As defined by IDEA, serious emotional disturbance includes schizophrenia but does not apply to children who are diagnosed as "socially maladjusted," unless it is determined that a serious emotional disturbance is also involved. The problems must occur over a long time, and the severity must be to a marked degree. (*Note*: The federal government is currently reviewing the way in which serious emotional disturbance is defined; the definition may be revised.)

Incidence

Estimates of the prevalence of emotional disorders in children vary widely because no standard and reliable definition or screening instrument exists. While numerous studies indicate that 6 to 10 percent of all school-aged children exhibit serious and persistent emotional/behavioral difficulties, according to the U.S. Department of Education (2001), only about 1 percent of schoolchildren in this country are identified as seriously emotionally disturbed. Even at this low estimate, however, we are talking about at least 400,000 children.

Characteristics

The causes of emotional disturbance have not been fully or precisely determined. Although various factors—such as heredity, brain disorder, diet, stress, and family functioning—have been suggested as possible causes and associated factors, research has not shown any of these factors to be the direct cause of emotional-behavioral problems.

Some of the characteristics and behaviors seen in children who have emotional disturbances may include the following:

- Acting out
- Aggressive, cruel, malicious, or assaultive behavior; fighting with peers
- Antisocial behavior (e.g., lying, stealing, vandalizing)
- Excessive anxiety
- Appearance of laziness, preoccupation, and lack of interest
- Attempted self-injury
- Attempts to injure others
- Attentional problems
- Defiance, fighting with authority figures, not following rules
- Poor social skills (e.g., trouble making friends)
- Appearance of deriving little enjoyment from school
- Impulsivity

- Inability to carry on normal routines
- Inappropriate behaviors
- Learning problems (e.g., performing academically below grade level)
- Low self-esteem
- Overdependence on adults
- Depression
- Threats of suicide or reported thoughts of suicide
- Lack of dependability
- Use of offensive language
- Making threats to try to get his own way

Children with the most serious emotional disturbances may exhibit distorted thinking, excessive anxiety, bizarre motor acts, abnormal mood swings, and hallucinations. These children may sometimes be identified (or misidentified) as having severe psychosis or schizophrenia.

While many children who do not have emotional disturbances may display some of the behaviors listed at various times during their development, a child with a serious emotional disturbance exhibits a number of these behaviors over long periods. Persistence of symptoms indicates the child is not coping with her environment or peers and may have a serious emotional disturbance.

Educational Implications

An educational program for a student with a serious emotional disturbance needs to help the child master academics; develop social skills; and increase self-awareness, self-esteem, and self-control. Career education (in the form of both academic and vocational programs) is also a major part of secondary education and should be a part of every child's transition plan, as outlined in his IEP.

Classroom Management Strategies

General Considerations

1. Plan for many breaks during the course of the day. The child with an emotional disability becomes drained very easily, burning out

more quickly than average, requiring frequent rest periods to "recharge" emotionally and, sometimes, physically.

2. Use a kind but firm tone of voice, avoiding harshness. The child needs to know what she is doing well rather than be punished for poor behavior. In addition, if the poor behavior stems from anxiety, increasing the child's anxiety with a harsh approach will be counterproductive.

3. Plan your daily schedule(s) and routines carefully. The child is likely to have trouble adjusting quickly to changes in routine or structure. Keep in mind the fewer transitions, the better. Warn the child whenever a change in schedule or routine is expected, giving him time to prepare himself.

4. Set daily, weekly, and monthly schedules. This gives the student a sense of security and predictability.

5. If you are not able to warn the child of a change in schedule or routine, kindly but firmly express your belief that the child can still cope. For example, you might say in a reassuring, matter-of-fact tone, "I know you weren't expecting this, Louis, but we'll get through it together."

6. Keep the classroom clean, neat, and well-organized. A dirty and disorganized classroom may convey that you do not have control of or care about the child's environment.

Student-Teacher Interaction

7. Plan a regular time, or "miniconference," during which you allow the child to speak to you freely without an audience. Giving the child a scheduled opportunity to state his concerns will help him learn not to act them out. It will also allow you to delay discussion of difficult issues to the scheduled time. If you react calmly to what the child has to say, not taking anything personally, you will build the child's trust, improving his behavior and academic performance.

8. Offer other behavioral options and explain that any inappropriate behavior is the child's decision. Making the child aware that behavior is his responsibility allows him to recognize that *not* doing something inappropriate is also in his control.

9. Preempt inappropriate behavior by waiting outside the door before class to tell the child in private what you expect during class. Also remind him of the consequences of his actions, both positive and negative. Consider arranging at the first miniconference you have with the child a few key, brief words with which

to greet him each morning (elementary) or before each class period (secondary).

10. Praise the child not only for complying with the rules but also for carrying out directions without "back talk" or other resistance.

11. Do not wait for scheduled miniconferences if you note that the child is becoming agitated. Instead, ask him if anything is bothering him. Such an opportunity, even if he refuses to tell you anything, may reduce his need for "spotlight" behaviors in front of the class.

12. Along the same lines, learn the child's nonverbal signals of impending upset. Ask former teachers, parents, special education consultants, and other school support staff to help you learn these as quickly as possible. For example, the child may talk to herself more, pace more, or begin to echo other's statements.

13. If lacking, teach the child an emotional vocabulary so she is better able to name her feelings, instead of inappropriately verbalizing or acting them out. The intense emotions a child with an emotional disability feels are very frightening, especially if she does not know how to label them. Empowering her to appropriately label and express her feelings may help her limit or control her fear and frustration. She will learn that saying "I'm angry" instead of calling names or kicking someone gets a more positive response from you.

Academic Considerations

14. Work out a contract with the child in which you allow him to choose the rewards he will receive for completing his work.

15. Make sure the curriculum and materials you present are compatible with the child's learning abilities. Frustration with work that is too hard or too easy may cause inattention.

16. Give shorter but more frequent assignments, promoting feelings of success instead of overwhelming the child.

17. Do not force the child to write if her handwriting is illegible or if she finds writing by hand a significant source of stress. Allow her to compensate with a word processor (e.g., see about voice recognition software), typewriter, or dictation buddy.

18. Correct and return assignments as soon as possible to reduce anxiety and give immediate positive reinforcement.

19. Reward the student for handing in neat, completed, and timely assignments. Be very specific, however, by what you mean by "neat," "organized," and so on.

20. Help the student get organized by keeping very little in his desk, using a spiral-bound notebook to keep pages together or large folders for him to keep work in, and so on.

21. Encourage the student to participate actively in classroom activities. Otherwise, the child may feel isolated and unwanted by teachers and peers. In addition, an uninvolved child has more time to worry and misbehave.

22. A child with emotional issues may also have other academic concerns. These include, but are not limited to, the following: gaps in learning (e.g., the child can solve complex math problems in his head but does not know his math facts); uneven acquisition of knowledge due to lengthy absences from school; delayed reading due to high anxiety; if gifted, inability to reach potential due to emotional limitations.

Behavior Management Considerations

23. Establish classroom rules and expected behaviors at the beginning of the year, and explain your reasons for having these rules. Limit the number of rules to four or five, however, making them easier to remember and enforce consistently.

24. Quiz the child individually to ensure he understands the rules, leaving less room for him to distort, deny, or rationalize what he believes he heard when you set the rules.

25. Give each class member and family a written copy of the rules. In addition, give the child a written copy of the rewards, positive feedback, and negative consequences for keeping or breaking the rules. Tape these copies of the rules, rewards, and consequences to the top of the child's desk as a constant reminder.

26. Stay close to the child whenever possible. This "proximity control" will help her stay on task. Seat her close to your desk or stand near her during a lesson.

27. Praise the student when he follows rules and pays attention. However, be aware that the child may have a hard time accepting praise, especially in front of a group. So do this in private. For younger children, praise and reward other students for following the rules. This method is known as *pinpointing*. Used

appropriately and not excessively, this will help the child notice appropriate models of behavior, helping her change her own behavior.

28. Avoid power struggles. The child may have a hard time "saving face" and so frequently gets "caught," or stuck, in struggles with authority. An audience may make the child feel she must over-react. In private, confront and suggest alternative behaviors, and allow the child to have her say about your rules and sug-gestions. Accept the student's statements sincerely and without arguing, but restate the rules and reasons for them along with the expectation that the child will follow them. For example, you might say, "I hear that you would like to talk to yourself during a test; however, the rule states that you are to 'Maintain appropriate quiet.' During tests, this is silence. You may talk during station time as long as you use an 'indoor voice.'"

29. If staying seated at appropriate times is a problem, watch for a pattern when the child is more active. You can arrange an alter-native behavior that is more acceptable to you (e.g., sending her on an errand, letting her come up to your desk, or giving her a "stress ball" to squeeze) at these times. This will help the child channel her tension and remain in control.

30. Use an external control, such as an egg timer, to remind the child to control his behavior. Start with a short time (1 minute or less) and one very specific target behavior (e.g., not inter-rupting others), then gradually increase the length of time you are asking the child to control his behavior as he experiences success. If, as is likely, you cannot be with the child all the time, work closely on this skill during only one lesson a day, such as during a small reading group.

31. To help the child see school as an interesting place, encourage and help the child start a club in her area of greatest interest and make participation contingent upon good attendance and appropriate behavior.

32. Punctuality may be an issue with the child because anxiety and other strong emotions may be highest before transitioning to school in the morning. To help alleviate or prevent this prob-lem, plan a special activity in the morning to motivate the child to get to school on time. If needed, find a buddy to walk or wait at the bus stop with the child to encourage punctuality. Reward the child for being on time—for example, extra free time, a token (if you are using a token economy), a note home, a com-

pliment, a point system with which to "purchase" privileges, and so on.

33. Write and ask the child and his parents to sign a nightly contract, listing all the things he needs to do to make the morning easier to manage. Then reward the child when he brings you the signed, completed contract.

34. Privately keep or have the child keep a chart to show her pattern of punctuality and lateness. This makes it easier for the child to see her habits and harder for her to deny a pattern of tardiness.

35. Give one direction at a time, and make it as simple as possible.

36. Have the child chart his own patterns of behavior, for example, how well he pays attention and follows directions.

37. Seat the child near calm, reliable classmates, keeping her away from those who might set her off.

38. Arrange for a safe and supervised "chill place" the student may safely go to cool off when he notices he is getting upset. Give him a laminated "chill pass" to show you before he leaves the room. Praise him for staying in tune with his strong feelings and taking a "positive time-out" instead of exploding. If the student seems to abuse this privilege, discuss your concerns with him at the next miniconference, negotiate the number of times he may use the pass, and encourage him to reduce this number over time as he learns to cope through other positive means. The "chill place" may also serve as an optional work area with fewer distractions than the classroom.

39. For the child who is not yet able to give herself a positive time-out or who chooses not to, set up a time-out area in the classroom where you can still monitor her behavior. This will allow you to define the start and end of a time-out very clearly, placing you in full control of this consequence.

40. Ask the child questions at random to increase attentiveness. However, if this increases the child's anxiety level, use proximity control instead. Or use audiovisual aids (e.g., an overhead projector, a tape recorder, a computer) to increase attention.

41. Work with the student to develop a nonverbal cue with which to signal her before giving her directions or other important information.

Social Skills Development

42. Privately help the child role-play with another student so he can get feedback on his social choices from a peer.

43. Provide the child with a "toolbox" of responses and options for typical social situations. Develop a social toolbox using index cards so that the child can go back and see what behaviors worked in which situations.

44. Network among other school staff and community mental health care providers to find the child a social skills-building group of peers to join.

45. Arrange for a peer to guide the child through social situations. He may be more willing to model peer behavior.

46. Initially, have the child work with only one partner for small group activities. Slowly increase the size of the group as the child becomes more socially adept and comfortable. Set up goal-oriented projects where students must work together to accomplish a task.

47. Have the child and a responsible peer organize team activities or group projects. The child may rise to the occasion when placed in a leadership role.

48. Praise the student as often as you genuinely can for positive rather than aggressive or otherwise inappropriate social behavior.

49. Systematically help the child develop positive relationship skills. While you may view certain "unwritten rules" as simple common sense, the child may lack understanding of and experience in basic social skills. Therefore, at least initially, a more direct rather than trial-and-error approach may be more effective.

Organizations

American Academy of Child and Adolescent Psychiatry
Public Information Office
3615 Wisconsin Avenue, NW
Washington, DC 20016–3007
202–966–7300
800–333–7636
Web site: www.aacap.org

Federation of Families for Children's Mental Health
1101 King Street, Suite 420
Alexandria, VA 22314
703–684–7710
Web site: www.ffcmh.org
E-mail: ffcmh@ffcmh.org

National Alliance for the Mentally Ill (NAMI)
Colonial Place Three
2107 Wilson Boulevard, Suite 300
Arlington, VA 22203–3042
703–524–7600
800–950–NAMI
TTY: 703–516–7227
Web site: www.nami.org
E-mail: helpline@nami.org

National Mental Health Association
1021 Prince Street
Alexandria, VA 22314–2971
703–684–7722
800–969–6642
TTY: 800–433–5959
Web site: www.nmha.org
E-mail: infoctr@nmha.org

Research and Training Center on Family Support
    and Children's Mental Health
Portland State University
P.O. Box 751
Portland, OR 97207–0751
800–628–1696
503–725–4040
Web site: www.rtc.pdx.edu
E-mail: rtcinfo@rripdx.edu

References and Bibliography

Adamec, C. (1996). *How to live with a mentally ill person: A handbook of day-to-day strategies.* New York: Wiley.

Breen, M. J., & Fiedler, C. R. (1996). *Behavioral approach to assessment of youth with emotional/behavioral disorders: A handbook for school-based practitioners.* Austin, TX: PRO-ED.

Brooks, B., & Sabatino, D. (1996). *Personal perspectives on emotional disturbances and behavioral disorders.* Austin, TX: PRO-ED.

Children's Hospital of Philadelphia. (1994). *A parent's guide to childhood and adolescent depression.* New York: Dell.

Eggert, L. L. (1994). *Anger management for youth: Stemming aggression and violence.* Bloomington, IN: National Education Service.

Gutkind, L. (1993). *Stuck in time: The tragedy of childhood mental illness.* New York: Holt.

Hatfield, A. B. (1991). *Coping with mental illness in the family: A family guide* (rev. ed.). Arlington, VA: National Alliance for the Mentally Ill.

Hatfield, A. B., & Lefley, H. P. (1993). *Surviving mental illness: Stress, coping, and adaptation.* New York: Guilford.

Jordan, D. (1995). *Honorable intentions: A parent's guide to educational planning for children with emotional or behavioral disorders.* Minneapolis: PACER Center.

Jordan, D. (1996). *What help can I expect from the school district for my child with an emotional or behavioral disorder? A parent's guide to service.* Minneapolis: PACER Center.

Kauffman, J. M. (1997). *Characteristics of emotional behavioral disorders of children and youth* (6th ed.). New York: Prentice Hall.

Koplewicz, H. S. (1996). *It's nobody's fault: New hope and help for difficult children.* New York: Times.

National Alliance for the Mentally Ill. (1996). *Resource catalog: A listing of resources from the National Alliance for the Mentally Ill* (rev. ed.). Arlington, VA: Author.

Sabatino, D. A., & Brooks, B. L. (1998). *Contemporary interdisciplinary interventions for children with emotional/behavioral disorders.* Durham, NC: Carolina Academic.

U.S. Department of Education. (2000). *Twenty-second annual report to Congress on the implementation of the Individuals with Disabilities Education Act.* Washington, DC: Author.

Whelan, R. J. (1997). *Emotional and behavioral disorders.* Denver: Love.

CHAPTER 4

Speech and Language Disorders

Definition

Speech and language disorders are problems with communication and related areas. Specifically, *speech disorders* involve difficulties producing speech sounds or problems with voice quality, whereas *language disorders* involve impairment in the ability to understand and/or use words in context, whether orally or in the form of sign language.

These challenges range from simple sound substitutions to an inability to understand or use language or the oral-motor mechanism for speech and feeding. Causes include, but are not limited to, hearing loss, neurological disorders, brain injury, developmental disability, prenatal drug abuse, and physical impairments (e.g., cleft lip or palate). Frequently, however, the cause is unknown.

Incidence

More than one million of the students served in public school special education programs are categorized as having a speech or language impairment. This estimate does not include children who have speech and language problems secondary to other conditions, such as deafness, developmental disabilities, autism, or cerebral palsy. More broadly, researchers estimate communication disorders (including speech, language, and hearing disorders) affect one of every ten people in the United States.

Characteristics

You should consider a child's communication to be delayed when the child is noticeably behind her peers in acquiring speech and/or language skills. Sometimes a child will have greater receptive (understanding) than expressive (speaking) language skills, but not always.

Speech Disorders

Speech disorders may involve the way the child forms sounds (*articulation* or *phonological disorders*) or may involve difficulties with the pitch, volume, or quality of the voice (*voice disorders*). A child may also have a combination of several problems. Trouble using some speech sounds may also be a symptom of a developmental delay. For example, a child may say "see" when he means "ski" or he may have trouble using certain sounds (e.g., "l" or "r"). Not surprisingly, you may have trouble understanding what the child is trying to say.

Three common types of speech disorder are stuttering, articulation disorders, and voice disorders.

- **stuttering**—An interruption in the rhythm of speech characterized by hesitations; repetitions; or prolongations (drawing out) of sounds, syllables, words, or phrases

- **articulation disorders**—Difficulties with the way sounds are formed and strung together, usually characterized by substituting one sound for another

- **voice disorders**—Inappropriate pitch (too high, too low, never changing [monotone], or interrupted by inappropriate breaks); loudness (too loud or not loud enough); or quality (harsh, hoarse, breathy, or nasal)

Additional characteristics of a speech disorder may include the following:

- Sounds develop more than a year later than peers
- Does not seem to have friends at preschool or grade school levels
- Problems with fluency (dysfluency) in the flow or rhythm of speech
- Inadequate vocabulary
- Difficulties with arithmetic
- Long pauses between words
- Consistent articulation errors (not age-appropriate)

- Talking too fast for speech to be clear

- Using mostly vowel sounds

Language Disorders

Language disorders include improper use of words and their meanings, inability to express ideas, inappropriate grammatical patterns, reduced vocabulary, and inability to follow directions. A child may have one or a combination of these characteristics if she has a *language learning disability* or *developmental language delay*. For example, a child may hear or see a word but not be able to understand its meaning. She may have trouble getting others to understand what she is trying to communicate.

Two language disorders are delayed language and aphasia.

- **delayed language**—A noticeable slowness in the development of the vocabulary and grammar necessary for expressing and understanding thoughts and ideas

- **aphasia**—The loss of speech and language abilities resulting from stroke or head injury

Additional characteristics of a language disorder may include the following:

- Poor concept formation

- Inadequate vocabulary

- Difficulty conveying messages or conversing with others

- Difficulty expressing personal needs

- Frustration from not being understood much of the time

- Trouble learning to read

- Inability to match sounds to letters

Educational Implications

Because all communication disorders may isolate individuals from their social and educational surroundings, it is essential to provide appropriate and timely intervention. While many speech and language patterns may be called "baby talk" and are part of a young child's normal development, they can become problems if they are not outgrown as expected. Indeed, if the problem is ignored beyond acceptable age ranges, an initial delay in speech and language or an initial incorrect speech pattern can become a disorder that may cause learning difficulties. Because of the way the brain develops, as a rule of thumb, it is easier to learn language and communication skills before the age of 5. Therefore, be sure to have children with muscular disorders, hearing problems, developmental delays, or any other potentially inhibiting factor fully evaluated to determine how, if, and to what degree their acquisition of speech, language, and related skills are affected.

Communication has many components, both verbal and nonverbal. All serve to increase the way individuals learn about the world around them, use knowledge and skills, and interact with colleagues, family, and friends. Not surprisingly, then, speech and language impairment may greatly impact a child's school and learning experience.

Classroom Management Strategies

General Considerations

1. Allow for breaks throughout the day. The child may use more energy during the school day to succeed and therefore need frequent chances to "recharge."

2. Be flexible. Understand the child may not be able to move or comprehend as quickly as others.

3. Be spontaneous with praise. Give it often, but genuinely, so it does not come across as mechanical or forced.

4. Create a relaxed communication environment by using short pauses between responses. Wait after speaking to give the child more processing time; this helps the student focus and concentrate on what you said.

5. Set rules for courteous conversation in which no student may interrupt another and all students must take turns.

6. Create an atmosphere of acceptance. Let the student know you are aware of the problems he is experiencing and are completely supportive.

7. Create situations in which the student must make choices, encouraging her to verbalize her needs and wants.

8. Encourage an environment that promotes verbal language. For example, refrain from jumping in too quickly to reduce the child's discomfort and anxiety.

9. Keep language simple when appropriate. Avoid being condescending, but use smaller words rather than larger ones that may confuse the child.

10. Be well-organized. The child needs clear routines and structure to perform best.

11. Keep the classroom clean and neat, sending a nonverbal message you are in control and care about the child's environment.

12. Place materials within view but out of reach to motivate verbal requests.

13. Set up activity centers that encourage the child to use verbal skills. Allow all students to take turns visiting these to talk about a variety of issues and topics and to discuss thought-provoking questions you have provided.

14. Set realistic goals, neither overchallenging nor underchallenging the child.

15. Enrich your classroom with a plethora of materials the child finds interesting to stimulate her to use speech and language skills.

Student-Teacher Interaction

16. Ask questions that require the child to speak in full sentences rather than use single-word answers. For example, instead of asking, "Do you like ice cream?" for which yes or no are likely answers, ask, "What kinds of ice cream do you like (please answer me by starting with 'I like')."

17. When working with the child one on one, ask him to verbalize his answers rather than write them down.

18. Encourage the child to talk about personal experiences so she will develop and use her vocabulary more often.

19. Lead class discussions about topics of interest to the child.

20. If the child is shy about speaking in front of the class, try alternate methods of presentation (e.g., videotaping the child's presentation) to help him feel more comfortable.

21. Listen attentively to the student. Focus closely on what she is saying, even if she is difficult to understand. This also provides a model of good listening.

22. Model good language skills. If you expect the child to use proper grammar and full sentences, you must do the same.

23. Provide the student with very clear guidelines about what you expect in your classroom (in written, verbal, or pictorial form).

24. Take extra time to promote self-confidence and self-esteem so the child does not feel nervous about speaking. Create successful experiences for the child to help him develop a positive self-image.

25. Don't exaggerate, but talk more slowly when addressing the child.

26. Build trust and therefore increase learning by understanding the child's strengths and weaknesses. Capitalize on the strengths, and try to avoid putting too much, if any, emphasis on the weaknesses.

27. When the student makes a mistake, model the correct form rather than correcting the mistake directly. For example, if the child says, "I want a waisin," you could respond with, "Here is a raisin; good job using a whole sentence!" instead of "It's *raisin*, not *waisin*."

Academic Considerations

28. Create situations in which you remove specific items, forcing the student to ask for the missing materials. For example, call on the child to write something on the chalkboard but purposely have no chalk handy so he must ask for it.

29. Evaluate work on the basis of gain or improvement, not on specific mastery levels. This will help promote a sense of success and accomplishment.

30. Allow more time to finish tests and assignments. Usually this accommodation is written into the IEP. Even if it is not, however, see if it helps the student complete more work and be more successful.

31. Give the student credit for effort, not only accomplishment.

32. Give the student extra time to think about an answer before actually speaking. This will help him gather his thoughts, possibly making speech easier.

33. Keep interesting and fun learning materials in the classroom. Choose activities that will motivate the student.

34. Incorporate activities that allow the child to practice what she has learned in speech therapy. To do this, keep in close contact with the speech therapist, and stay up to date as to the progress and limitations of the student.

35. Teach concepts in ways that speak to many different senses. For example, use overhead projectors, audio- and videotape

recorders, movies, computers, interactive games, manipulative objects, and so on.

36. Break down assignments into smaller units to increase the chances of success.

37. Foster a high degree of participation from the student, encouraging her to become involved in classroom activities. This will increase learning and decrease feelings of isolation.

38. Use cooperative learning strategies to promote learning. This will also reinforce speech and language development through peer interaction.

39. Use personal stories from your own and the student's experiences to make learning more interesting and "real-world." For example, have the child dictate a story about his favorite game or toy.

40. The child may have difficulty understanding instructions or attending to new information. Repeat instructions and lessons as necessary.

41. If the child seems easily distracted, deliver information in small chunks.

42. Watch for problems with short-term memory. If evident, avoid giving multistep directions.

Social Skills Development

43. Create an environment in which you encourage all children to communicate with one another. This requires careful planning and organization on your part.

44. Create situations that involve students in small groups, and provide other opportunities for teamwork.

45. Create a roundtable discussion center at which all students may talk freely in small groups about a topic of your choosing.

46. Have the student work with a partner. They can help each other, repeating words to each other and pronouncing them clearly.

47. Teach the student about appropriate positive relationships and the value of making friends with others.

48. Understand that the child may not know the unspoken rules of conversation and social interaction that most of us take for granted. This often leads to inappropriate behavior with peers, making it difficult for the child to make or keep friends. The

combination of academic failure and social failure can lead to low self-esteem and fear of further failure. Consequently, the child may need to be systematically and deliberately taught social cues and graces.

Organizations

Alliance for Technology Access
2175 E. Francisco Boulevard, Suite L
San Rafael, CA 94901
415–455–4575
800–455–7970
Web site: www.ataccess.org
E-mail: atainfo@ataccess.org

American Cleft Palate–Craniofacial Association (ACPA)
104 S. Estes Drive, Suite 204
Chapel Hill, NC 27514
919–933–9044
800–242–5338
Web site: www.cleftline.org
E-mail: cleftline@aol.com

American Speech–Language–Hearing Association (ASHA)
10801 Rockville Pike
Rockville, MD 20852
301–897–5700 (voice/TTY)
ASHA Answer Line: 888–321–ASHA (888–321–2742; toll-free)
ASHA Action Center: 800–498–2071
Web site: www.asha.org
E-mail: actioncenter@asha.org

Division for Children with Communication Disorders
c/o Council for Exceptional Children
1920 Association Drive
Reston, VA 22091–1589
703–620–3660
888–CEC–SPED (888–232–7733; toll-free)
TTY: 703–264–9446
Web site: www.cec.sped.org
E-mail: service@cec.sped.org

Easter Seals (National Office)
230 W. Monroe Street, Suite 1800
Chicago, IL 60606

312–726–6200
800–221–6827
TTY: 312–726–4258
Web site: www.easter-seals.org
E-mail: info@easter-seals.org

Learning Disabilities Association of America (LDA)
4156 Library Road
Pittsburgh, PA 15234–1349
412–341–1515
888–300–6710 (toll-free)
Web site: www.ldanatl.org
E-mail: ldanatl@usaor.net

Scottish Rite Foundation
Southern Jurisdiction, USA, Inc.
1733 Sixteenth Street NW
Washington, DC 20009–3103
202–232–3579
Web site: www.srmason-sj.org

Trace Research and Development Center
University of Wisconsin-Madison
5901 Research Park Boulevard
Madison, WI 53705–1252
608–262–6966
TTY: 608–263–5408
Web site: trace.wisc.edu
E-mail: web@trace.wisc.edu

References and Bibliography

Berkowitz, S. (1994). *The cleft palate story: A primer for parents of children with cleft lip and palate.* Chicago: Quintessence.

Bernthal, J. E., & Bankson, N. W. (1993). *Articulation and phonological disorders* (3rd ed.). Englewood Cliffs, NJ: Prentice Hall.

Beukelman, D. R., & Mirenda, P. (1992). *Augmentative and alternative communication: Management of severe communication disorders in children and adults.* Baltimore: P. H. Brookes.

Eisenson, J. (1997). *Is my child's speech normal?* (2nd ed.). Austin, TX: PRO-ED.

Hamaguchi, P. M. (1995). *Childhood speech, language, and listening problems: What every parent should know.* New York: Wiley.

Kersner, M., & Wright, J. A. (1996). *How to manage communication problems in young children.* London: David Fulton.

Kreplin, E., & Smith, B. (1997). *Sound and articulation activities for children with speech-language problems.* New York: Prentice Hall.

Mannix, D. (1997). *Oral language activities for special children.* New York: Prentice Hall.

Romski, M. A., & Sevcik, R. A. (1996). *Breaking the speech barrier: Language development through augmented means.* Baltimore: P. H. Brookes.

Schetz, K. F., Taylor, P. G., & Cassell, S. K. (1996). *Talking together: A parent's guide to the development, enrichment, and problems of speech and language.* Blacksburg, VA: Pocahontas Press.

Wright, J. A. (1998). *Supporting children with communication problems: Sharing the workload.* London: David Fulton.

CHAPTER 5

Hearing Impairments

Definition

The IDEA specifically includes *hearing impairment* and *deafness* as two of the categories under which children with disabilities may be eligible for special education and related service programming. While laypeople and professionals alike may use the term "hearing impairment" generically to describe a wide range of hearing losses, including deafness, IDEA defines the two terms separately:

- **hearing impairment**—An impairment in hearing, whether permanent or fluctuating, that adversely affects a child's educational performance

- **deafness**—A hearing impairment that is so severe that the child is impaired in processing linguistic information through hearing, with or without amplification

In other words, a child is considered *deaf* if his hearing impairment severely reduces his ability to process language through hearing, with or without amplification, and if his hearing impairment greatly affects his educational performance. A child is considered *hearing impaired* if his hearing impairment affects his ability to process language through hearing to a lesser degree than if he were considered deaf, whether the impairment is permanent or fluctuating, and if his hearing impairment adversely affects his educational performance, but to a lesser degree than if he were deaf.

In short, a child who is deaf cannot receive sound in all or most of its forms. A child with a hearing impairment, or loss, can respond to some sound ("auditory stimuli"), including speech.

Incidence

Hearing impairment and deafness may occur at any time from infancy through old age. The U.S. Department of Education (2000) reports that, during the 1998–1999 school year, 70,813 students aged 6 to 21 (or 1.3 percent of all students with disabilities) received special education services under the category of "hearing impairment." However, the number of children with hearing loss and deafness is undoubtedly higher because many of these students may have other disabilities as well that are served under other categories.

Characteristics

There are four types of hearing loss, any of which may cause hearing impairment or deafness.

Conductive hearing losses are caused by diseases or obstructions in the outer or middle ear, which are the pathways along which sound is conducted to the inner ear. Conductive hearing losses usually affect all frequencies of hearing evenly and do not result in severe losses. A child with a conductive hearing loss is usually able to use a hearing aid well or can be helped with medication or surgery.

Sensorineural hearing losses result from damage to the delicate sensory hair cells of the inner ear or the nerves that serve the inner ear. Severity may range from mild to profound. This type of hearing loss often affects the person's ability to hear certain frequencies more than others. Thus, even with amplification to increase the sound level, a child with a sensorineural hearing loss may perceive distorted sounds, sometimes making it impossible to use a hearing aid successfully.

A *mixed* hearing loss is a combination of conductive and sensorineural losses, affecting both the outer or middle and the inner ear.

A *central* hearing loss results from damage to the nerves or neurons of the central nervous system, either in the pathways to the brain or in the brain itself.

Educational Implications

Generally, a child who is either hearing impaired or deaf requires some form of special education services to receive an appropriate education. Such services may include the following:

- ◆ Regular speech, language, and auditory training from a specialist

- ◆ Amplification systems

- An interpreter's services (if the student uses sign language)
- Seating favorable to speech-reading (formerly called *lipreading*)
- Captioned videotapes and television
- A note-taker's assistance (to help the child fully attend to and benefit from the instruction)
- Instruction for teacher(s) and peers in alternate communication methods, such as sign language
- Counseling (job or personal)

Classroom Management Strategies

General Considerations

1. Seat the child where he may see as many classmates as possible (especially their faces). For example, arrange the desks in a semicircle.

2. Ask all students to speak clearly and distinctly.

3. Make sure the classroom is well-lit so your face is illuminated, allowing the student to speech-read more accurately.

4. Keep in mind the child may become fatigued more quickly than other children her own age.

5. Place the child away from areas where noise may be a serious distractor.

6. Don't exaggerate, but speak more slowly and enunciate words more carefully.

7. Encourage the child to turn around to watch the faces of classmates who are speaking.

8. Find out what type of hearing aid/auditory trainer the child uses and how it works.

9. Use your hands when speaking to help the student better understand what you are explaining.

Student-Teacher Interaction

10. If the child's hearing impairment involves only one ear or is greater in one ear than the other, seat the child in the front corner seat with the ear with greater hearing toward you. In any case, seat the child as close to you as possible.

11. Face the child as much as possible, even when speaking to the whole class.

12. Encourage the child to watch your face whenever you are speaking.

13. Speak—and encourage peers to speak—naturally, using natural gestures and staying face to face with the child. Do not speak loudly or exaggerate lip movements.

14. Pay attention to the tilt of the child's head. The habits of extending the head or twisting the neck to hear better may become firmly fixed, stressing the neck and spinal column. Adjust the child's physical position so she doesn't have to contort herself to hear.

15. Whenever possible, have your mouth at the child's eye level when speaking.

16. If you suspect the child is struggling (either socially or academically), avoid guessing what is wrong. Be very direct, asking the child if you can help.

17. Provide support, and validate the student's feelings. Be open, and let the student vent in a controlled, private setting.

18. Be consistent and predictable when dealing with problems. The student needs to see you as a good "lifeguard" and an "anchor" during difficult times.

Academic Considerations

19. When possible, the child should have a note-taker. This helps the child focus on the instruction by allowing her to watch you carefully without the distraction of taking notes.

20. Give short, concise instruction, and privately have the student repeat the key points to ensure you communicated effectively.

21. List all key points on the chalkboard.

22. Allow more time to finish tests and assignments. Usually, this accommodation is already listed in the child's IEP. Even if it is not, however, see if it helps the child perform better.

23. Foster an interest in music and singing. Feeling the variety of vibrations can enhance the child's understanding of music and sound.

24. As often as possible, write (or, as appropriate, help the child write) the details of class and homework assignments to ensure

the child understands the requirements, then double-check for understanding.

25. Be patient with the child's communication process.

26. Use several forms of communication (e.g., sign language, speech, visual aids, and the like) to clarify all concepts you are teaching.

27. Be aware that gaps in learning are common. Do not get frustrated. Your frustration may make the child feel as if the problems are her fault.

28. During reading lessons, appoint the child a peer buddy. Direct this student to point out who is reading aloud and what part of the text the reader is on.

29. Encourage the child to participate actively in lessons that encourage verbal expression, such as reading aloud, conversation, storytelling, and creative dramatics.

30. Encourage the child to ask to have statements repeated when he does not understand what someone is saying. Check for understanding, and be patient when repeating yourself. Encourage peers to be patient and understanding.

31. Most television shows and many videotapes are closed captioned for the hearing impaired. Arrange to have a television or video system that can make use of this.

32. Liberally decorate your classroom with colorful artwork (both professionally and student-produced) and posters to provide stimulation the child does not receive through sound.

33. If the student is young, label items in the classroom to help him develop a broader vocabulary.

34. Outline the day's schedule on the chalkboard so the student knows what will be happening throughout the day.

35. The student may not always know how words fit together to make understandable sentences. Help her develop these skills by always writing and speaking in complete, grammatically correct sentences.

Social Skills Development

36. Establish a partnership between the child and a classmate who is compassionate, patient, and mature. This will help the child feel more connected to peers. Initially, choose the classmate

carefully, providing appropriate training, guidance, and supervision. Seat the child next to this student.

37. Teach the child about appropriate positive relationships and the value of making friends with others.

38. Create opportunities for small group work and other teamwork activities. Children without disabilities can be excellent models of appropriate behavior and social interaction to help the child assimilate into regular educational settings.

39. A child who trusts you will behave better and learn more. Build trust by taking the time to allow the child to express her feelings about whatever she is going through that day.

40. Observe the child carefully to ensure he doesn't withdraw or otherwise suffer emotionally as a direct or indirect result of his hearing challenge.

41. Create an environment in which you encourage all children to communicate with one another clearly, patiently, and respectfully.

42. Have a roundtable discussion center at which all students may talk freely in groups about a topic of your choosing. Encourage the child to participate.

43. Include the child fully in all plays and other social opportunities that develop oral communication skills.

44. Understand the child may not know the unspoken rules of conversation and social interaction that most of us take for granted. This often leads to inappropriate interactions with peers, making it difficult for the child to make or keep friends. The combination of academic failure and social failure can lead to low self-esteem and fear of further failure. Consequently, you may need to teach the child social cues and graces systematically and deliberately.

Organizations

Alexander Graham Bell Association for the Deaf
3417 Volta Place NW
Washington, DC 20007–2778
202–337–5220
TTY: 202–337–5221
Web site: www.agbell.org
E-mail: info@agbell.org

American Society for Deaf Children
P.O. Box 3355
Gettysburg, PA 17325
717–334–7922
800–942–ASDC (800–942–2732; voice/TTY)
Web site: www.deafchildren.org
E-mail: asdc1@aol.com

American Speech–Language–Hearing Association (ASHA)
10801 Rockville Pike
Rockville, MD 20852
301–897–5700 (voice/TTY)
ASHA Answer Line: 888–321–ASHA (888–321–2742; toll-free)
ASHA Action Center: 800–498–2071
Web site: www.asha.org
E-mail: actioncenter@asha.org

National Deaf Education Network and Clearinghouse
Laurent Clerc/National Deaf Education Center
Gallaudet University
KDES PAS 6
800 Florida Avenue NE
Washington, DC 20002–3695
202–651–5051 (voice/TTY)
Web site: clerccenter.gallaudet.edu
E-mail: clearinghouse.infotogo.gallaudet.edu

National Institute on Deafness and Other Communication Disorders
National Institutes of Health
One Communication Avenue
Bethesda, MD 20892–3456
800–241–1044
TTY: 800–241–1055
Web site: www.nidcd.nih.gov
E-mail: nidcdinfo@nidcd.nih.gov

Self Help for Hard of Hearing People (SHHH)
7910 Woodmont Avenue, Suite 1200
Bethesda, MD 20814
301–657–2248 (voice)
301–913–9413 (TTY)
Web site: www.shhh.org
E-mail: national@shhh.org

References and Bibliography

Biderman, B., & Thomas, W. (1998). *Wired for sound: A journey into hearing.* Grawn, MI: Trifolium.

Carlton, J. (1999). *Frames and lenses.* Thorofare, NJ: Slack.

Carmen, R. (1998). *Consumer handbook on hearing loss and hearing aids: A bridge to healing.* Sedona, AZ: Auricle Ink.

Clark, J., & Martin, F. (1996). *Hearing care for children.* Boston: Simon & Schuster.

Dugan, M. B., & Dugan, M. P. (1997). *Keys to living with hearing loss.* Hauppuage, NY: Barrons Educational Series.

Flexer, C. (1994). *Facilitating hearing and listening in young children: Early childhood intervention series.* San Diego: Singular.

Glickman, N. S., & Harvey, M. A. (1996). *Culturally affirmative psychotherapy with deaf persons.* Hillsdale, NJ: Erlbaum.

Heidinger, V. A. (1996). *Analyzing syntax and semantics: A self-instructional approach for teachers and clinicians.* Washington, DC: Gallaudet University.

Lane, H. L., Hoffmeister, R., Bahan, B., & Machemer, C. (1996). *A journey into the deaf-world.* San Diego: Dawn Sign.

Marsh, C. (1999). *Ear's looking at you, kid! A look at you and your hearing impairment.* Peachtree City, GA: Gallopade.

Martini, A., Read, A., & Stephens, D. (1996). *Genetics and hearing impairment.* San Diego: Singular.

Matkin, N., & Rousch, J. (1994). *Infants and toddlers with hearing loss: Family-centered assessment and intervention.* Baltimore: York.

Medwig, D. J., & Weston, D. C. (1995). *Kid-friendly parenting with deaf and hard of hearing children: A treasury of fun activities toward better behavior.* Washington, DC: Gallaudet University.

Murray, N. T. (1994). *Let's converse: A how-to guide to develop and expand conversational skills of children and teenagers who are hearing impaired.* Washington, DC: Alexander Bell Association for the Deaf.

Pappas, D. G. (1998). *Diagnosis and treatment of hearing impairment in children.* San Diego: Singular.

Ross, M. (Ed.). (1990). *Hearing-impaired children in the mainstream.* Parkton, MD: York.

Schwartz, S. (1996). *Choices in deafness: A parent's guide to communication options.* Bethesda: Woodbine.

Suss, E. (1999). *When the hearing gets hard: Winning the battle against hearing impairment.* Secaucus, NJ: Citadel.

U.S. Department of Education. (2000). *Twenty-second annual report to Congress on the implementation of the Individuals with Disabilities Education Act.* Washington, DC: Author.

Wayner, D. S. (1998). *Hear what you've been missing: How to cope with hearing loss—Questions, answers, options.* New York: Wiley.

CHAPTER 6

Visual Impairments

Definition

Visual impairment is the consequence of a functional (physical) loss of vision rather than an *eye disorder* itself. Eye disorders that may lead to visual impairments include retinal degeneration, albinism, cataracts, glaucoma, muscular problems, corneal disorders, diabetic retinopathy, congenital disorders, and infection. In the educational context, the terms *partially sighted, low vision, legally blind,* and *totally blind* are used to describe the various types of visual impairments a student may have. Each type may be defined as follows:

- **partially sighted**—Indicates that some type of visual problem has resulted in a need for special education (less severe than *low vision*).

- **low vision**—Generally refers to a severe visual impairment, not necessarily limited to distance vision. Low vision applies to all children who have sight but are unable to read the newspaper at a normal viewing distance, even with the aid of corrective lenses. A child with low vision uses a combination of vision and other senses to learn, although he may require adaptations in lighting or the size of print and, sometimes, Braille text.

- **legally blind**—Indicates children with less than 20/200 vision in the better eye or a very limited field of vision (20 degrees at its widest point), even with corrective lenses. Individuals who are legally blind learn through senses other than sight, such as touch (e.g., Braille).

- **totally blind**—Describes children with no measurable vision. Individuals who are legally blind learn through senses other than sight, such as touch (e.g., Braille).

Incidence

The rate at which visual impairments occur in individuals under the age of 18 is 12.2 per 1,000. Severe visual impairments (legally or totally blind) occur at a rate of .06 per 1,000, or 6 per 100,000 (National Information Center for Children and Youth with Disabilities, 2001).

Characteristics

The impact of visual problems on a child's development depends on the severity of the loss, type of loss, age at which the condition appeared, and overall level of functioning of the child. Many children who have multiple disabilities may also have visual impairments that delay motor, cognitive, and/or social development.

A young child with visual impairments has little reason to explore interesting objects in her environment and, thus, may miss opportunities to have experiences from which to learn. This lack of exploration is likely to continue until learning becomes motivating or until intervention begins.

In addition, because the child cannot see parents or peers, she may be unable to imitate social behavior or receive and understand nonverbal cues. In short, visual impairments can create obstacles to a growing child's learning and independence.

Characteristics of a child with a visual impairment may include the following:

- Blinking forcefully and/or more than usual
- Inability to perceive facial expressions or respond appropriately to expressions
- Cloudy vision
- Delayed fine and gross motor skills
- Delayed language development
- Difficulty copying, writing, or performing other visual-motor tasks
- Difficulty using charts, maps, or diagrams
- Inability to see objects to one side or the other (poor peripheral vision)
- Light sensitivity
- Tilting of head
- Walking cautiously

Educational Implications

To benefit from early intervention programs, a child with, or suspected of having, a visual impairment should be diagnosed and assessed as soon as possible after birth or suspicion. The child may need special equipment and modifications to the regular curriculum to help her develop listening, communication, and orientation and mobility skills; vocational/career options; and activities of daily living (ADL) skills. A student with low vision or who is legally blind may need help learning to use her residual vision more efficiently and to work with special aids and materials. For a student with a visual impairment combined with one or more other disabilities, a more thorough interdisciplinary approach is appropriate, with emphasis on self-care and ADL skills.

Classroom Management Strategies

General Considerations

1. Ensure the classroom is well-lit so your face is illuminated, allowing the student to see you clearly.

2. Acquaint the child with her surroundings in each school environment (e.g., the classroom, the art room, the cafeteria, the playground).

3. Set up a private study area for the student outside the regular classroom, so if, for example, he needs to have more quiet, he has a positive and safe place to go with appropriate supervision.

4. Inform the student of any changes in routine ahead of time to allow him to plan for adjustments.

5. Keep in mind that the child may become fatigued more quickly than other children his own age.

6. Keep the child away from areas where noise may be a serious distraction. She needs to be able to use her hearing fully.

7. Seat the child next to a student with no visual impairment. Encourage the other student to help the child as needed.

8. While the child may need help functioning fully in the school setting, work to prevent the child's becoming too dependent on others. Look for ways to foster independence.

9. Speak naturally, use natural gestures, and face the student when communicating. Encourage other students to do the same. Avoid overacted and potentially condescending communication styles.

10. Along the same lines, do not speak loudly or allow classmates to do so. Remember, the child has a visual impairment, not a hearing impairment.

11. Learn the appropriate body positioning for the child's form of visual impairment and for various types of classroom activities. This will help you maximize the child's potential and abilities.

12. Encourage the child to turn around to watch (as is possible) the faces of other children who are speaking. Help the child learn to position herself face to face with others.

13. Likewise, encourage the child to face you and watch (as is possible) your face whenever you are speaking.

14. Arrange other students around the child so he can see as many classmates as possible.

15. Do not tolerate obnoxious behavior or rude comments from other students. Model and demand respect for all students.

16. For the child with some vision, gesture to express visually what you are explaining with your hands when speaking within the child's visual distance limit.

17. When going through a door with the student, always go ahead of him, telling him which way the door opens.

Physical Accommodations

18. Be sure there are grab bars and nonskid mats where needed in the bathroom.

19. Direct classmates to be sure to clean up around them so nothing remains on the floor to trip over.

20. Remove any other obstacles that could be a danger to the child. This includes eliminating protruding and overhanging objects the child may bump into.

21. Explain to the other students the importance of pushing their chairs in when they get up.

22. Place needed materials on shelves easily accessible to the student.

23. If the child's visual impairment involves only one eye, or if the impairment is greater in one eye than the other, seat the child in the front corner seat with the eye that has greater vision toward you.

24. Hang coat hangers in a position suitable for all so the child does not feel different from others.

25. If any furniture has been rearranged in the classroom, be sure to inform the child before he enters the room.

26. Add a "talking clock" to your classroom.

27. If the child has a guide dog, be sure the classroom is set up for maximum efficiency for the animal. Consult the child's parents or other experts if needed.

28. To ensure you are following school policy and to best protect the student, be sure to go over all emergency exit procedures and plans (e.g., fire drills) with both the student and your administration.

29. Do not seat the child in direct or strong sunlight; this may create more visual distortion.

30. If possible, depending on the specific disability involved, schedule classes on the first floor where access to everything will be easier.

31. Arrange the desks in a semicircle, with classmates as close to the child as possible to give the child a better view of them when they speak.

32. Investigate the possibility of installing guide ropes in your classroom and perhaps to and from other areas in the school (e.g., cafeteria, gymnasium).

33. Obtain large-print books and other materials for the child, if appropriate.

34. Provide thicker pens and pencils.

Academic Considerations

35. Provide a teaching assistant or peer to take notes for the child. This will allow the child to listen more carefully with fewer distractions.

36. Arrange for a personal reader for the child.

37. Give short, concise instructions, then have the student repeat them to check for understanding.

38. Allow additional time for taking tests and doing assignments, whether or not this accommodation is in the child's IEP. See if it improves the child's performance.

39. Provide a tape recorder to help the child review lessons outside of class.

40. Tap into school and community resources to set up the student with a voice-activated word processor to use in class. Provide headphones as well when appropriate.

41. As often as possible, write down and say page numbers, home-work assignments, and the like to ensure the child understands the requirements of each assignment. Then double-check for understanding.

42. Clearly explain all concepts you are teaching by using several forms of communication (e.g., three-dimensional art, sound/music, manipulative materials such as math counters, and the like).

43. Arrange to have texts converted into Braille with the use of a machine-optacon. This machine "reads" typed text and changes it into a tactile experience through pins that rise and fall while the student "reads" them with her fingers. Or investigate the use of *Versabraille*, which can convert material received by a computer into Braille. Computer printouts or files can also be converted into speech with a Kurzweil Reading Machine.

44. Describe the child's wider environment using creative imagery, helping to orient the child to this environment.

45. Gaps in learning are common for the child with a visual impair-ment. Do not express frustration with this. Doing so will likely make the student feel guilty.

46. During reading lessons, appoint a peer buddy for the child. Teach the buddy how to point out discreetly who is reading and what part of the text the reader is on.

47. Through adaptive materials, encourage the child to take an active interest and participate fully in expressive activities, such as reading, conversation, storytelling, and creative dramatics. These activities offer the opportunity for positive experiences.

48. Make or obtain age-appropriate magazines and books the child may enjoy. (*Note:* Some children's magazines and many popular books are available both in Braille and on audiotape through the Library of Congress; see the National Library Service for the Blind and Physically Handicapped under the "Organizations" section of this chapter.)

49. For the child with some sight, decorate the entire classroom colorfully—for example, with three-dimensional art, bright posters, and child-produced items.

50. Work hard to stimulate the child's other senses and abilities (e.g., hearing and touch)—whatever it takes to help her under-stand what she cannot see.

51. Manipulatives are effective tools for teaching beginning math skills to elementary students. Abacus beads are particularly use-

ful to the student with a visual impairment for counting, adding, and subtracting.

52. Always read the daily schedule aloud to help the student keep track of what will be happening.

53. Teach the student listening skills. Do not assume that simply because he has a visual impairment he is automatically a good listener.

54. Use large paper on an appropriate easel to draw large pictures, diagrams, and so on. Place the easel as close to the student as is needed.

55. Let the student touch real objects in natural settings so she can learn about shape, size, weight, hardness, texture, pliability, temperature, and other characteristics of the physical world.

56. Provide a talking calculator.

57. Mix visual activities with auditory and motor activities whenever possible. For example, have small groups act out and verbalize a story you just read aloud.

58. When the child is reading in Braille, have her read aloud to you.

59. When writing on the chalkboard, be sure to make your letters, numbers, and diagrams large.

Student-Teacher Interaction

60. Always address the child by name before asking her any questions.

61. Seat the child in the front of the room as close as possible to you.

62. We cannot emphasize enough that you and the child's classmates should always talk in a normal tone of voice. A visual impairment does not imply a hearing or other disability; this assumption can easily be conveyed by tone and volume of your voice, hampering the student's ability to trust you—and believe in herself.

63. Whenever you leave the student, always let him know you are doing so.

64. Beyond this, if the visual impairment is severe, help the child learn to trust you by letting her know where you are at all times in the classroom.

65. Discreetly ask the child if she can see what you are doing.

66. When speaking to the child, try to make sure your mouth is at the child's eye level so the child has a "perfect" view of what you are saying.

67. Face the child as much as possible, even when speaking to the whole class.

Organizations

American Council of the Blind
1155 15th Street NW, Suite 1004
Washington, DC 20005
202–467–5081
800–424–8666
Web site: www.acb.org
E-mail: info@acb.org

American Foundation for the Blind
11 Penn Plaza, Suite 300
New York, NY 10001
800–AFB–LINE (800–232–5463; hotline)
Publications: 800–232–3044
Web site: www.afb.org
E-mail: afbinfo@afb.net

Blind Children's Center
4120 Marathon Street
Los Angeles, CA 90029–3584
323–664–2153
800–222–3566 (outside California)
800–222–3567 (in California)
Web site: www.blindcntr.org
E-mail: info@blindcntr.org

Division for the Visually Handicapped
Council for Exceptional Children
1920 Association Drive
Reston, VA 22091–1589
703–620–3660
888–CEC–SPED (888–232–7733; toll-free)
TTY: 703–264–9446
Web site: www.cec.sped.org
E-mail: service@cec.sped.org

The Foundation Fighting Blindness
    (formerly National Retinitis Pigmentosa Foundation)
Executive Plaza One, Suite 800
11350 McCormick Road
Hunt Valley, MD 21031–1014
410–785–1414
888–394–3937 (toll-free)
TTY: 410–785–9687 or 800–683–5551
Web site: www.blindness.org

National Association for Parents of Children with Visual Impairments
P.O. Box 317
Watertown, MA 02471
617–972–7441
800–562–6265
Web site: www.spedex.com/napvi

National Association for Visually Handicapped
22 West 21st Street
New York, NY 10010
212–889–3141
Web site: www.navh.org
E-mail: staff@navh.org

National Braille Association, Inc. (NBA)
3 Townline Circle
Rochester, NY 14623–2513
716–427–8260
Web site: members.aol.com/nbaoffice
E-mail: nbaoffice@compuserve.com

National Braille Press
88 St. Stephen Street
Boston, MA 02115
617–266–6160
888–965–8965 (toll-free)
Web site: www.nbp.org

National Eye Institute
National Institutes of Health
U.S. Department of Health and Human Services
2020 Vision Place
Bethesda, MD 20892–3655
301–496–5248
Web site: www.nei.nih.gov

National Federation of the Blind
1800 Johnson Street
Baltimore, MD 21230
410–659–9314
Web site: www.nfb.org
E-mail: nfb@nfb.org

National Library Service for the Blind and Physically Handicapped
Library of Congress
1291 Taylor Street NW
Washington, DC 20542
202–707–5100
800–424–8567
TDD: 202–707–0744
Web site: www.loc.gov/nls
E-mail: nls@loc.gov

Prevent Blindness America
500 E. Remington Road
Schaumburg, IL 60173
708–843–2020
800–331–2020
Web site: www.prevent-blindness.org
E-mail: info@preventblindness.org

References and Bibliography

American Foundation for the Blind. (1998). *AFB directory of services for blind and visually impaired persons in the United States* (25th ed.). New York: Author.

Barraga, N. C., & Erin, J. N. (1992). *Visual handicaps and learning.* Austin: PRO-ED.

Best, A. B. (1997). *Teaching children with visual impairments.* New York: Taylor and Francis.

Blakely, K., Lang, M. A., Kushner, B., & Iltus, S. (1995). *Toys and play: A guide to fun and development for children with impaired vision.* Long Island City, NY: Lighthouse.

Carlton, J. (1999). *Frames and lenses.* Thorofare, NJ: Slack.

Corn, A. L., & Huebner, K. M. (1998). *A report to the nations: The national agenda for the education of children and youths with visual impairments, including those with multiple disabilities.* New York: American Foundation for the Blind.

Curran, E. P. (1988). *Just enough to know better: A Braille primer.* Boston: National Braille.

Ferrell, K. A. (1996). *Reach out and teach: Materials for parents of visually handicapped and multihandicapped young children.* New York: American Foundation for the Blind.

Ferrin, D. M. (1997). *Guide to resources for children and youth with visual impairments.* Westminster, CA: Cane and Corn.

Haring, N. G., & Romes, L. T. (1995). *Welcoming students who are deaf-blind into typical classrooms: Facilitating school participation, learning and friendship.* Baltimore: P. H. Brookes.

Harrison, F., & Crow, M. (1993). *Living and learning with blind children.* Toronto: University of Toronto Press.

Holbrook, M. C. (1996). *Children with visual impairments: A parent's guide.* Bethesda: Woodbine.

National Information Center for Children and Youth with Disabilities. (2001). *Visual impairments* (Fact Sheet No. 13). Washington DC: Author.

Nicholson, L. (1996). *Helen Keller: Humanitarian.* New York: Chelsea House.

O'Connor, K., Erin, J., Kay, J. L., Chen, D., Lewis, S. et al. (1998). *Skills for success: A career education handbook for children and adolescents with visual impairments.* New York: American Foundation for the Blind.

Pierce, B. (1995). *The world under my fingers: Personal reflection on Braille.* Baltimore: National Federation for the Blind.

Sacks, S. Z., & Silberman, R. K. (1998). *Educating students who have visual impairments with other disabilities.* Baltimore: P. H. Brookes.

Scott, E., Jan, J., & Freeman, R. (1995). *Can't your child see?* (2nd ed.). Austin: PRO-ED.

Smith, M., & Levack, N. (1996). *Teaching students with visual and multiple impairments: A resource guide.* Austin: TSBVI.

Torres, I., & Corn, A. (1990). *When you have a visually handicapped child in your classroom: Suggestions for teachers.* New York: American Foundation for the Blind.

Warren, D. H. (1994). *Blindness and children: An individualized approach.* Cambridge, MA: Brookline.

Webster, A., & Roe, J. (1998). *Children with visual impairments: Social interaction, language, and learning.* New York: Routledge.

CHAPTER 7

Orthopedic and Other Health Impairments

Definition

Two main terms describe the disabilities discussed in this chapter: *orthopedic impairment* and *other health impairment* (OHI).

Orthopedic Impairment

The IDEA defines *orthopedic impairment* as follows:

> A severe orthopedic impairment . . . includes impairments caused by anomaly (e.g., club foot, absence of some member), impairments caused by disease (e.g., bone tuberculosis) and impairments from other causes (e.g., cerebral palsy, spina bifida).

In contrast, many local and state agencies and special educators use the term *physical disabilities* when referring to the same students described by the IDEA definition. Later in this chapter, we will further divide orthopedic impairment into *neuromotor impairment* and *musculoskeletal conditions,* for the purpose of providing a more detailed outline of the types and characteristics of specific disabilities.

Other Health Impairment

Under the IDEA, the term *other health impairment* is defined as follows:

> Having limited strength, vitality, or alertness due to chronic or acute health problems such as a heart condition, tuber-

culosis, rheumatic fever, nephritis, asthma, sickle cell anemia, hemophilia, seizure disorder, lead poisoning, leukemia, or diabetes that adversely affects a child's educational performance.

This is a "catch-all" category for physical conditions that may create disability but that do not have another official designation.

Incidence

Researchers gather statistics according to the categories just defined.

Orthopedic Impairment

According to the U.S. Department of Education (2000), only about half a percent of school-aged children have physical disabilities. Thus, approximately 200,000 children with physical disabilities need special education in the United States.

Other Health Impairment

About 1 percent of, or about 400,000, students are served by schools under IDEA's OHI category. In addition, another 3 percent or so of, or 1.2 million, students have some type of health impairment that is not debilitating enough to qualify them for special education under IDEA.

Characteristics

Orthopedic Impairment

Neuromotor Impairment

Neuromotor refers to the way the nervous (neuro) system controls the muscular system (motor). Several conditions describe how this vital relationship may be impaired in an individual.

Cerebral Palsy

This condition is characterized by paralysis, weakness, poor neuromotor coordination, and other motor dysfunction because of damage to the brain before it has matured. The following are the major types of cerebral palsy (CP):

- **diplegia**—The legs are paralyzed to a greater extent than the arms.

- **hemiplegia**—One half of the body is paralyzed.

♦ **paraplegia**—Both legs are paralyzed.

♦ **quadraplegia**—All four limbs are paralyzed.

Classification of CP can also be divided into three types of brain damage:

♦ **pyramidal cerebral palsy**—Results in stiffness of muscles and poor voluntary movement.

♦ **extrapyramidal cerebral palsy**—Involuntary movements and floppiness of the muscles are evident.

♦ **mixed cerebral palsy**—Damage creates a mixture of effects (e.g., elasticity in the legs but rigidity in the arms).

Seizure Disorder: Epilepsy

Children with epilepsy have recurrent seizures or sudden changes of consciousness caused by abnormal discharges of electrical energy in the brain. Children with epilepsy may experience various types of seizures:

♦ **generalized**—Seizure involves a large portion of the brain.

♦ **partial seizure**—Seizure begins in a localized area and involves only a small part of the brain.

♦ **absence seizure**—Seizure causes a short lapse in consciousness; also known as a *petit mal* seizure.

♦ **tonic-clonic**—Formerly known as a *grand mal* seizure; characterized by a stiff phase (tonic) followed by a jerking phase (clonic) in which the arms and legs will "snap."

Multiple Sclerosis

A chronic disease typically occurring in adults in which transmissions of electrical signals from the spinal cord to the brain begin to deteriorate. As with muscular dystrophy, health care needs center on lung function support, prevention of pneumonia, and physical therapy.

Muscular Dystrophy

A hereditary disease characterized by progressive weakness caused by degeneration of muscle fibers. Health care needs center on lung function support, prevention of pneumonia, and physical therapy.

Polio

This condition is caused by a viral infection but, fortunately, is almost totally prevented in the United States by immunization. Polio attacks the spinal cord and may result in paralysis and other motor disabilities.

Spina Bifida

This is a congenital problem caused by failure of the bony spinal column to close completely during fetal development. Because the spinal column is open, the spinal cord may protrude, resulting in damage to the nerves, paralysis, and/or lack of function or sensation below the site of the defect. This protrusion of the spinal column is called *myelomeningocele.*

Musculoskeletal Impairment

Another large group of conditions that may cause mild to severe disability involve the musculoskeletal system of the body, which coordinates movements between the muscles and the bones. Here we describe the most common conditions found in children.

Arthritis

What people typically call arthritis may take various forms:

- **juvenile arthritis**—Involves the inflammation of the joints.

- **osteoarthritis**—The most common form of arthritis among children with disabilities; movement is painful or impossible because of damage to the cartilage around the joint.

- **rheumatoid arthritis**—The most common form of arthritis among adults; a systematic disease with major symptoms involving the muscles and joints.

Skeletal Disorders and/or Limb Anomalies

Several specific conditions fit this category, including the following:

- **club foot**—One or both feet turned at the wrong angle at the ankle

- **scoliosis**—Abnormal curvature of the spine

- **Legg-Calve-Perthes disease**—Flattening of the head of the femur (the thighbone where it inserts into the pelvis to form the hip joint)

- **osteomyelitis**—Bacterial infection of the bone

- **arthrogryposis**—Muscles of the limbs missing or smaller and weaker than normal

- **osteogenesis imperfecta**—Bones formed improperly, breaking very easily

Other Health Impairments

Here, we look more closely at the OHIs that form a loosely linked category of disabilities under IDEA.

AIDS

AIDS, or Acquired Immune Deficiency Syndrome, is caused by a virus that breaks down the immune system. There is no known cure, although treatment may prolong and improve the quality of life.

Asthma

This chronic respiratory condition is characterized by repeated episodes or difficulty in breathing, especially with exhalation.

Cancer

Cancer is a very broad term that may describe any of a multitude of types of abnormal growth of cells, affecting any organ or other body system.

Cystic Fibrosis

This inherited disease is characterized by chronic respiratory and digestive problems, including thick, sticky mucus and glandular secretions.

Diabetes

This form of diabetes is a hereditary or developmental problem of sugar metabolism caused by the failure of the pancreas to produce enough insulin. Referred to as *Type II diabetes,* this form occurs in adulthood.

Juvenile-Onset Diabetes

Juvenile-onset diabetes develops when the pancreas stops producing or produces too little of the hormone insulin. When this happens, the blood cells do not absorb glucose, and unused sugar builds up in the blood. Juvenile-onset diabetes is often referred as *Type I diabetes.*

This disease usually develops before the age of 35, and it occurs most commonly in young people between the ages of 10 and 16— hence its name. The onset is rapid, and without injections of insulin, the child will become comatose and die.

Hemophilia

This is a rare, hereditary disorder of males in which the blood does not have a sufficient clotting component and excessive bleeding occurs.

Nephrosis

This is a noninflammatory disease of the kidneys, involving deficiency of albumin in the blood.

Rheumatic Fever

This often recurrent illness involves painful swelling and inflammation of the joints that can spread to the brain or heart.

Sickle Cell Anemia

This term describes a severe, chronic hereditary blood disease in which red blood cells are distorted in shape and do not circulate properly.

Tuberculosis

Tuberculosis involves infection by the tuberculosis bacterium of an organ system, such as the lungs, heart, joints, and so on.

Educational Implications

Educational programs for the child with orthopedic impairment or other health impairment should include mastering academics; developing social skills; and increasing self-awareness, self-esteem, and self-control. In addition, at the secondary level, career education (both academic and vocational programs) and life-skills planning should be major parts of every adolescent's transition plan, as outlined in the IEP.

Classroom Management Strategies

General Considerations

1. Establish a partnership between the child and an understanding and compassionate classmate. This peer can help the child locate classes, follow schedules, and the like.

2. If the child needs attention from the school nurse, allow her to leave the classroom without having to explain why at that time.

3. Be patient when activities take much longer than expected.

4. Be sure to go over all emergency exit procedures and plans with the student and the administration (so you are sure of school policy for ensuring the student's safety).

5. Contact the parents to find out what interests the child. Whenever possible, incorporate the child's interests into the curriculum.

6. Encourage the child's classmates to focus on the child's abilities, not disability.

7. Explain rules and expectations to the child to eliminate confusion. Give him and his family written copies of the rules.

8. Find out from both the parents and school administration what your role should be regarding dressing or toileting the child. Also respectfully discuss this with the child so that she neither feels uncomfortable nor embarrassed.

9. Arrange for a private, supervised study area for the student outside the regular classroom so he may have privacy and quiet as needed.

10. Frequently evaluate the student's needs and progress to ensure you are modifying the student's program as necessary.

11. As needed and appropriate, inform the child's classmates about the child's needs. Be sure, however, to consult with the child's parents and to respect family wishes and rights to privacy. Prepare the class through lectures, guest speakers, literature, and so on. If possible, have the child and his parents help with this process.

12. Minimize visual and auditory distractions in the room. When helpful, use a study carrel or other work center to limit extraneous stimuli.

13. Without exaggerating, speak at a relatively slow pace, with appropriate pauses for processing time. Repeat information as needed.

14. Provide cues to help the child prepare for transitions, such as "In 10 minutes, we will be going to the gymnasium."

15. Provide two sets of books, one for home and one for school. This will make life easier for the student and family, while decreasing any anxiety about carrying heavy books home.

16. Read and learn about the disability. Become knowledgeable and empathetic as to what the child is experiencing.

17. Remember that the child may become more fatigued than other children.

18. Set up one notebook for the student to use in all subjects so she has less to manipulate and carry. Use a solid pad or spiral-bound notebook rather than loose pieces of paper to help keep materials organized and to reduce frustration.

19. Make sure the student is positioned so she can hear and see you and as many classmates as possible. In addition, if the child is in a wheelchair, learn about appropriate body positioning for maximal breathing and speaking capabilities.

20. Do not tolerate obnoxious behavior or rude comments from other students. Inform the students on the first day of school you will take such behavior toward anyone very seriously. Inform students of the consequences for breaking this rule.

21. Understand the student may need more bathroom trips than other students may.

Physical Accommodations

22. If the child uses a wheelchair, make sure your classroom is wheelchair accessible. For example, check that doors and aisles are wide enough.

23. Be sure the bathroom is accessible and has grab bars, raised toilet seat(s), and nonskid mats.

24. Be sure all ramps are clear of obstacles.

25. Provide the child with a supervised place where he can lie down and rest, if the need should arise.

26. Have railings aligning the walls of the classroom in place for support.

27. Depending on the disability involved, try to schedule classes on the first floor, where access to everything will be easier.

28. Place materials on shelves easily accessible to the student.

29. Keep the room arrangement, materials available, and routines as consistent as possible. Whenever possible, inform the child of any changes ahead of time.

30. Offer rubber thimbles to help with page-turning.

31. Provide the student with thicker pens and pencils.

32. If the child cannot hold a book, give her a book stand.

33. Use adaptive materials (e.g., a lap board) to modify the angle of the student's desk.

34. Provide age- and ability-appropriate large-print books, visual guides, and books on tape.

Academic Considerations

35. Allow the student to tape-record lessons to help him with visual-motor coordination, handwriting difficulties, and the like.

36. Provide a computer with appropriate software (e.g., a voice recognition program).

37. As appropriate, give oral exams and more time for tests and assignments, including homework. Give untimed exams, if the child's disability impacts his reading or writing ability. Whether or not the IEP already lists these accommodations, keep in mind they may greatly improve the child's performance, especially if they reduce anxiety level.

38. Allow the student to copy your notes or, if appropriate, photocopy your notes for her. At a minimum, provide written outlines of key points and instructions.

39. Keep written instructions simple, and offer them frequently.

40. Find activities that help develop the child's gross motor skills. Ask the physical therapist for ideas. For this and fine motor skills, also ask the parents and child what the child likes to do to help motivate him.

41. Likewise, include activities that promote fine motor skills. Ask the child's physical therapist for ideas. Age-appropriate arts and crafts activities (e.g., stringing beads, playing with clay, or cutting with scissors) are excellent for improving fine motor coordination.

42. Wait long enough for the student to respond. Certain physical disabilities may create processing problems.

43. Ask the school psychologist or special education consultant and get the family's permission to consult with medical personnel involved with the child about how to monitor thought-processing skills.

44. Help the student learn how to structure her thinking process graphically through time lines, flowcharts, and graphs.

45. Make sure the student who also has a visual impairment can see your mouth whenever you are speaking. Covering your mouth may create anxiety and communication problems in the child.

46. Give the student extra attention when appropriate. Provide frequent and immediate feedback.

47. If possible, have the child keep a daily journal of assignments. If needed, give the child a written list of assignments, instead of requiring him to write these down. Either method (if appropriate) fosters self-confidence as well as shows the student one way to organize and prepare.

48. Give the student a written set of questions before she reads any material so she knows what to read for.

49. Show the student how to use an index card to help her with scanning and keeping her place while reading.

50. Teach the student how to highlight text and make notations when reading long passages.

Social Skills Development

51. Use the student partnership you have established to help the student feel more connected to peers and included in the classroom. Initially, be very careful whom you select to better facilitate this process.

52. Create opportunities for work in small groups to help the student make friends, learn and hone social skills, and allow classmates to get to know the person behind the disability.

53. Not only does small group learning help the child academically, it also increases social skills. Interactions with children without disabilities and peer-modeling of target behaviors are crucial for assimilation into the regular classroom.

54. Take time to listen to the child, allowing her time to express feelings about whatever she is going through at any given time.

55. Along the same lines, avoid guessing what is wrong if you suspect a problem. Be very direct, asking the child if you can be of any assistance.

56. Provide support and validate the student's feelings. You must be open and let the student vent in a controlled setting. This may require private time alone with the child.

57. Be consistent and predictable when dealing with problems. The student needs to see you as a good "lifeguard," capable of giving dependable help during difficult times.

Organizations

American Cancer Society
Georgia/Southeast Division, Inc.
2200 Lake Boulevard
Atlanta, GA 30319
404–816–4994
800–ACS–2345 (800–227–2345)
Web site: www.cancer.org

American Diabetes Association
1701 N. Beauregard Street
Alexandria, VA 22313
800–DIABETES (800–342–2383)

Arthritis Foundation
Georgia Chapter
550 Pharr Road, Suite 550
Atlanta, GA 30305
404–237–8771
800–933–7023
Web site: www.arthritis.org
E-mail: info.ga@arthritis.org

Epilepsy Foundation of America
4351 Garden City Drive
Landover, MD 20785
301–459–3700
800–332–1000

March of Dimes Birth Defects Foundation
1275 Mamaroneck Avenue
White Plains, NY 10605
914–428–7100
888–MODIMES (888–663–4637; toll-free)
Web site: www.modimes.org

Muscular Dystrophy Association
3300 E. Sunrise Drive
Tucson, AZ 85718
800–572–1717

National Association of People with AIDS
1413 K Street NW, 7th Floor
Washington, DC 20005
202–898–0414
Web site: www.napwa.org
E-mail: napwa@napwa.org

National Foundation for Asthma
1233 20th Street NW, Suite 402
Washington, DC 20036
202–466–7643
800–7–ASTHMA (800–727–8462)
Web site: www.aafa.org

Spina Bifida Association of America
4590 MacArthur Boulevard NW, Suite 250
Washington, DC 20007–4226
202–944–3285
800–621–3141

United Cerebral Palsy Associations
1660 L Street NW, Suite 700
Washington, DC 20036–5602
202–776–0406
800–872–5827
TTY: 202–973–7197
Web site: www.ucp.org
E-mail: webmaster@ucp.org

References and Bibliography

Appleton, R., & Gibbs, J. (1998). *Epilepsy in childhood and adolescence.* Malden, MA: Blackwell Science.

Bellenir, K. (1997). *Congenital disorders sourcebook: Basic information about disorders acquired during gestation, including spina bifida, hydrocephalus, cerebral palsy, heart defects, and craniofacial abnormalities.* Detroit: Omnigraphi.

Betschart, J. (1999). *Diabetes care for babies, toddlers, and preschoolers: A reassuring guide.* New York: Wiley.

Broughton, N. S., & Menelaus, M. B. (1998). *Menelaus' orthopedic management of spina bifida cystica.* Philadelphia: Saunders.

Carson, M. K. (1998). *Epilepsy.* Springfield, NJ: Enslow.

Colbert, D. (1999). *Diabetes.* Lake Mary, FL: Creation House.

Dormans, J. P., & Pellegrino, L. (1998). *Caring for children with cerebral palsy: A team approach.* Baltimore: P. H. Brookes.

Geralis, E. (1998). *Children with cerebral palsy: A parent's guide.* Bethesda: Woodbine.

Guthrie, D. W., & Guthrie, R. (1999). *The diabetes sourcebook: Today's methods and ways to give yourself the best care.* Los Angeles: Lowell House.

Jerreat, L. (1999). *Diabetes.* San Diego: Whurr.

Lechtenberg, R. (1999). *Epilepsy and the family: A new guide.* Boston: Harvard University Press.

Lutkenhoff, M., & Oppenheimer, S. G. (1997). *Spinabilities: A young person's guide to spina bifida.* Bethesda: Woodbine.

Marshall, F. (1999). *Epilepsy: Practical and easy-to-follow advice.* Boston: Element.

Mecham, M. J. (1996). *Cerebral palsy.* Austin: PRO-ED.

Milchovich, S. K., & Dunn-Long, B. (1999). *Diabetes mellitus: A practical handbook.* Menlo Park, CA: Bull.

Miller, G., & Clark, G. D. (1998). *The cerebral palsies: Causes, consequences, and management.* Portsmouth, NH: Butterworth-Heinemann.

Mondesir-Itiaba, J. (1999). *Diabetes: Everybody's business.* New York: Vantage.

Sandler, A. (1997). *Living with spina bifida: A guide for families and professionals.* Chapel Hill: University of North Carolina.

Smith, T. (1999). *Diabetes.* New York: DK.

Touchette, N. (1999). *The diabetes problem solver.* Chicago: Contemporary.

U.S. Department of Education. (2000). *Twenty-second annual report to Congress on the implementation of the Individuals with Disabilities Education Act.* Washington, DC: Author.

CHAPTER 8

Traumatic Brain Injury

Definition

The IDEA defines *traumatic brain injury* (TBI) as follows:

> An acquired injury to the brain caused by an external physical force resulting in total or partial functional disability or psychosocial impairment, or both, that adversely affects a child's educational performance. The term applies to open or closed head injuries resulting in impairments in one or more areas, such as cognition; language; memory; attention; reasoning; abstract thinking; judgment; problem solving; sensory, perceptual, and motor abilities; psychosocial behavior; physical functions; information processing; and speech. The term does not apply to brain injuries that are congenital or degenerative or brain injuries induced by birth trauma.

In short, TBI is any brain injury caused by physical force instead of genetics, disease, or birth trauma.

Incidence

More than 100,000 children and youth between the ages of birth and 21 are hospitalized each year for head injuries. Estimates vary regarding the long-term effects of the injuries. Some researchers have found that 1 in 500 of these children develop persistent behavior problems, while others have found that over one-third of the injuries result in lifelong disabilities (National Information Center for Children and Youth with Disabilities, 2000). In general, about half the children and youth who experience TBI will require special education, and those who return to regular classes will require modifications to be successful.

Characteristics

Children with TBI may exhibit various symptoms, as outlined in the following sections.

Medical/Neurological Symptoms

Children with TBI may experience short- and long-term medical and neurological (nervous system-related) complications from the original injury, including the following:

- Sensory deficits affecting vision, hearing, taste, smell, or touch
- Concussion
- Skull fracture
- Decreased motor coordination
- Difficulty breathing
- Dizziness
- Headache
- Impaired balance
- Loss of intellectual capabilities
- Partial to full paralysis
- Poor eye-hand coordination
- Reduced body strength
- Seizure activity (possibly frequent)
- Sleep disorders
- Speech problems (e.g., stuttering, slurring)

Cognitive Symptoms

Children with TBI also tend to have many problems with thought processes necessary to learning and succeeding in school, including the following:

- Decreased attention
- Decreased organizational skills
- Decreased problem-solving ability
- Difficulties keeping up at school

- Difficulty with abstract reasoning
- Integration problems (e.g., sensory, thought)
- Poor organizational skills
- Memory deficits
- Perceptual problems
- Poor concentration
- Poor judgment
- Rigidity of thought
- Slowed information processing
- Poor short- and long-term memory
- Word-finding difficulty

Behavioral/Emotional Symptoms

Sometimes, the child also develops debilitating behavioral and emotional problems as a direct and an indirect result of the injury, including the following:

- Aggressive behavior
- Denial of deficits
- Depression
- Difficulty accepting and responding to change
- Loss or reduction of inhibitions
- Distractibility
- Feelings of worthlessness
- Flat affect (expressionless, lacking emotion)
- Low frustration level
- Unnecessary or disproportionate guilt
- Helplessness
- Impulsivity
- Inappropriate crying or laughing
- Irritability

Social Skills Development

Given the potential for behavioral and emotional symptoms, it should come as no surprise that a child with TBI may also have social skills issues, including the following:

- Difficulties maintaining relationships with family members and others

- Inability to restrict socially inappropriate behaviors (e.g., disrobing in public)

- Inappropriate responses to the environment (e.g., overreactions to light or sound)

- Insensitivity to others' feelings

- Limited initiation of social interactions

- Social isolation

Educational Implications

As mentioned earlier, roughly half of children and youth who experience traumatic brain injury will require special education, and those who return to regular classes will need accommodations to be successful. As an educator, you can play an important role in the recovery of the student with TBI, providing considerable assistance during and beyond the difficult adjustment period that returning to school creates.

Classroom Management Strategies

General Considerations

1. Establish and foster a partnership between the child and a classmate who is understanding and compassionate. Assign this peer or another peer to help the student find classes, follow schedules, and the like.

2. Allow the child to leave the classroom to visit the nurse without having to explain why at that time.

3. Be patient when activities take longer than expected. The child may have processing difficulties; if so, simply plan more time for lessons.

4. Be sure to go over all emergency exit procedures and plans with the student. Make sure you know the school administration's

guidelines as to the specific way you should keep the student safe.

5. Encourage classmates to focus on the child's abilities, instead of her disability.

6. Explain rules and expectations to the child to eliminate confusion. Provide her and her family with written copies of the rules.

7. Arrange for a private, supervised study area for the student outside of the regular classroom for him to use as needed. For example, if the student is especially overwhelmed by noise at a particular time, give him the option of choosing to work away from the class. Try to be sure your classroom environment does not force this to happen too often, isolating the student further.

8. Evaluate the student frequently, modifying the student's program as necessary.

9. As needed and appropriate, inform the child's classmates about the child's needs. Be sure, however, to consult with the child's parents and to respect family wishes and rights to privacy. Prepare the class through lectures, guest speakers, literature, and so on. If possible, have the child and her parents help with this process.

10. Minimize visual and auditory distractions in the classroom. When helpful, set up a study carrel or other work center to limit extraneous stimuli.

11. Without exaggerating, speak at a relatively slow pace, with appropriate pauses for processing time. Repeat information as needed.

12. Provide cues to help prepare the child for transitions (e.g., "In 15 minutes, we will be going to music class").

13. Provide two sets of books, one for home and one for school. This is a simple way to make life easier for the student and family while decreasing any anxiety about carrying heavy books home.

14. Remember the child may become fatigued more easily than her peers.

15. Set up one notebook for the student to use for all subjects so he has less to manipulate and carry. Use a solid pad or spiral-bound notebook rather than loose pieces of paper to help keep materials organized and reduce frustration.

16. Make sure the student can hear and see you and as many class-mates as possible during whole-group activities.

17. Do not tolerate obnoxious behavior or rude comments from peers. Let the class know on the first day of school you will take teasing and the like very seriously. Note what the consequences will be if this rule is violated.

Physical Accommodations

18. Be sure the bathroom is accessible, has grab bars, raised toilet seats, and nonskid mats.

19. Be sure ramps are installed where needed and kept clear of obstacles.

20. If necessary and possible, and depending on the specifics of the disability involved, schedule classes on the first floor where access to everything will be easier.

21. For the child who uses a wheelchair, make sure your classroom is wheelchair accessible. For example, check that the door and aisle widths allow easy maneuvering of the wheelchair.

22. Ask that your classroom be fitted with railings for support.

23. Air-conditioning in the classroom in hot and humid weather makes the environment more conducive to learning for all children, but especially for the child with TBI.

24. Place needed items on shelves easily accessible to the student. (*Note:* If the child is in a wheelchair, this will be quite different from what you may find easy.)

25. Keep the room arrangement, materials available, and routines as consistent as possible. Whenever you can, inform the child of any changes ahead of time.

26. Provide the child with a supervised place where she can lie down and rest, if the need should arise.

27. Offer rubber thimbles to help with page-turning.

28. Provide thicker pens and pencils to increase fine motor control.

29. If the child cannot hold a book, give him a book stand.

30. Use adaptive materials (e.g., a lap board) to modify the angle of the student's desk.

31. Provide age-appropriate large-print books, visual guides, and books on tape.

Academic Considerations

32. Allow the child to tape-record lessons to help her with visual-motor coordination challenges, handwriting difficulties, and the like.

33. Set up a computer for the student. With some help the student may be able to use a voice recognition program, research information by clicking away instead of turning pages, or do any of a number of other tasks.

34. As appropriate, give oral exams and more time for tests and assignments, including homework. Give untimed exams if the child's disability impacts his reading or writing ability. Whether or not the IEP already lists these accommodations, keep in mind they may greatly improve the child's performance, especially if they reduce his anxiety level.

35. As appropriate, give the student your notes to copy or a photocopy of your notes. At a minimum, provide written outlines of key points and instructions.

36. Keep written instructions simple, and offer them frequently.

37. Integrate meaningful arts and crafts and other fine motor activities into the curriculum. For example, when studying Native Americans, have your class make simple replicas of Native American art. Or, when studying simple addition, have the class count and place small objects into piles to represent the sums.

38. Ask a physical therapist to plan activities that promote gross motor skills. For example, have small groups act out a science concept or topic, such as a volcano erupting.

39. Wait long enough for the student to respond. Certain brain injuries may create processing challenges.

40. Monitor whether the student is thinking and processing appropriately. Ask the school psychologist or special education consultant to get the family's permission to consult with medical personnel involved with the child about how to monitor these skills.

41. Help the student structure his thinking process graphically by using time lines, flow charts, graphs, and other visual aids.

42. Provide written outlines for writing assignments. Create answer lines for the child to fill in, helping him learn the structure you are asking for.

43. Make sure the child who also has a visual impairment can see your mouth when you are speaking. Covering your mouth may create anxiety and communication problems in the child.

44. Have the child keep a daily journal of assignments. If needed, provide a list of the assignments instead of requiring the child to write them down. Keeping track of assignments fosters self-confidence as well as showing the child a way to organize and prepare.

45. Give the child extra attention when appropriate. Offer frequent and immediate feedback.

46. Give the child a written set of questions before he reads any material so he knows what to read for.

47. Show the student how to use an index card to help her with scanning and keeping her place while reading.

48. Teach the student how to highlight text and make notations when reading long passages.

Social Skills Development/Student-Teacher Interaction

49. Use the student partnership you established to help the child feel more connected to peers and included in the classroom. Initially, be very careful whom you select to facilitate this process.

50. Create opportunities for group work to help the child make friends, learn and hone social and communication skills, and allow classmates to get to know the person behind the disability.

51. Not only does small group learning help the child academically, it also increases social skills. Interactions with children without disabilities and peer modeling of target behaviors are crucial for assimilation into the regular classroom.

52. Take time to listen to the child, allowing her time to express feelings about whatever she is going through at any given time.

53. Along the same lines, avoid guessing what is wrong if you suspect a problem. Be very direct, asking the child if you can be of any assistance.

54. Provide support and validate the child's feelings. You must be open and let the student vent in a controlled setting. This may require private time alone with the child.

55. Be consistent and predictable when dealing with problems. The child needs to see you as a good "lifeguard" and anchor during difficult times.

Organization

Brain Injury Association
105 N. Alfred Street
Alexandria, VA 22314
703–236–6000
800–444–6443
Web site: www.biausa.org
E-mail: FamilyHelpline@biausa.org

References and Bibliography

Bigler, E. D., Clark, E., & Farmer, J. E. (1997). *Childhood traumatic brain injury: Diagnosis, assessment, and intervention.* Austin: PRO-ED.

Corbett, S. (1996). *Educating students with traumatic brain injuries: A resource and planning guide.* Madison: Wisconsin Department of Publications.

Green, B. S., Stevens, K. M., & Wolfe, T. D. (1997). *Mild traumatic brain injury: A therapy and resource manual.* San Diego: Singular.

Kreutzer, J. S., & Wehman, P. H. (1996). *Cognitive rehabilitation for persons with traumatic brain injury.* Bisbee, AZ: Imaginart.

Mira, M. P., Tucker, B. F., & Tyler, J. S. (1999). *Traumatic brain injury in children and adolescents: A sourcebook for teachers and other school personnel.* Austin: PRO-ED.

National Information Center for Children and Youth with Disabilities. (2000). *Traumatic brain injury* (Fact Sheet No. 18). Washington, DC: Author.

Stoler, D. R., & Hill, B. A. (1997). *Coping with mild traumatic brain injury.* Garden City Park, NY: Avery.

Varney, N. R., & Roberts, R. J. (1999). *The evaluation and treatment of mild traumatic brain injury.* Hillsdale, NJ: Erlbaum.

Winslade, W. J. (1998). *Confronting traumatic brain injury: Devastation, hope, and healing.* New Haven, CT: Yale University.

Ylvisaker, M. (1997). *Traumatic brain injury rehabilitation: Children and adolescents.* Portsmouth, NH: Butterworth-Heinemann.

CHAPTER 9

Developmental Disabilities

Definition

Formerly called *mental retardation*, the term *developmental disabilities* encompasses a range of conditions. Generally, a child with an intelligence test score of 70 or less and significant difficulty adjusting to everyday life is considered to have a developmental disability. The child develops at a below-average rate and has difficulty learning (e.g., reading, writing, activities of daily living) and adjusting socially. *Down syndrome* is the most common and readily identifiable chromosomal abnormality associated with developmental disability. For some unexplained reason, an accident in cell development results in 47 instead of the usual 46 chromosomes. The extra chromosome disrupts the orderly development of the body and brain. In most cases, the diagnosis of Down syndrome is made based on the results of a chromosome test administered shortly after birth.

Other causes of developmental disabilities include asphyxia (lack of oxygen), blood incompatibility between the mother and fetus, and maternal infections (e.g., rubella, herpes). Researchers have also linked certain drugs to developmental disabilities.

A developmental disability is not a disease, nor should it be confused with mental illness. Keep in mind, a child with a developmental disability does not remain a child; she becomes an adult. She *does* learn, but slowly and with difficulty.

Incidence

When both intelligence testing and the person's ability to adapt to everyday life are factored in, about 1 percent of the general population has a developmental disability (U.S. Department of Education,

2000). In the 1998–1999 school year, over 610,445 students aged 6 to 21 were classified as having a developmental disability and served by public schools, comprising 1.7 percent of the total school enrollment. These figures, however, do not include students with multiple disabilities or those in general (noncategorized) special education preschool programs who may also have a developmental disability.

Approximately 4,000 children with Down syndrome are born in the United States each year, or about 1 in every 800 to 1,000 live births. Although parents of any age may have a child with Down syndrome, the incidence is higher in mothers over age 35. Most common forms of Down syndrome do not usually occur more than once in a family, suggesting that the chromosomal change is random, not hereditary.

Characteristics

Some authorities believe that people with developmental disabilities develop in the same way as people without developmental disabilities but at a slower rate. Others suggest that people with developmental disabilities have distinct and lasting problems with basic thinking and learning skills, such as attention, perception, and/or memory. According to the latter theory, the child with a developmental disability will develop differently from peers without the disability with regard to academic, social, and vocational skills. To a great degree, severity of the impairment—mild, moderate, severe, or profound—dictates achievement.

There are over 50 clinical signs of Down syndrome, but it is rare to find all or even most of them in one person. Generally, individuals with Down syndrome have a flat face with low nose bridge, small nose, and almond-shaped eyes; are usually smaller than their nondisabled peers; and experience slower physical and intellectual development than peers.

In addition, a child with Down syndrome is likely to have specific health-related problems, including a lower resistance to infection, making him more prone to respiratory problems; visual problems such as crossed eyes and far- or nearsightedness; mild to moderate hearing loss; speech and language difficulties; heart defect (many types of which are now correctable); gastrointestinal tract problems (which may be surgically corrected); and obesity.

A child with Down syndrome may also have a condition known as *atlantoaxial instability*, a misalignment of the top two vertebrae of the neck. This condition makes the child more prone to injury when participating in activities that hyperextend or flex the neck. Urge parents to have their child examined by a physician to determine whether the child should be restricted from certain sports and other activities that place stress on the neck (e.g., gymnastics, football, dance). Although this misalignment is a potentially serious condition, proper diagnosis and precautions can help prevent serious injury.

Educational and Employment Implications

A child with a developmental disability may display abilities and potential within a very wide range. The following discussion includes an overview of this issue, then outlines the educational and vocational challenges and goals according to the severity of the disability.

Overview

Shortly after a diagnosis of Down syndrome or other developmental disability is confirmed, parents should be encouraged to enroll their child in an infant development/early intervention program. These programs offer parents special instruction in teaching their child language, cognitive, self-help, and social skills, as well as in practicing specific exercises for gross and fine motor development. Stimulation during early developmental stages improves the child's chances of developing to his or her fullest potential. Continuing education, positive public attitudes, and a stimulating home environment have also been found to promote the child's overall development.

As in the general population, in individuals with developmental disabilities, a wide range of intellectual abilities, behavior, and developmental progress exists. As mentioned earlier, the level of developmental delay may range from mild to severe, with the majority functioning in the mild to moderate range. The overall range possible makes predicting the future achievements of children with developmental disabilities extremely difficult.

Thus, it is important for families and all members of the IEP team to refrain from placing arbitrary limits on what they believe the child may ultimately achieve. Having said this, some general guidelines for teaching the child and promoting the child's independence in adulthood may be helpful:

- ◆ Emphasize concrete concepts rather than abstract ideas.

- ◆ Teach tasks step by step, with frequent reinforcement and consistent feedback.

- ◆ Keep in mind that improved public acceptance of persons with disabilities, along with increased opportunities for adults with disabilities to live and work independently in the community, has expanded the possibilities for children with Down syndrome and other developmental disabilities.

- Independent living centers, supervised group apartments, and other support services in the community have proven to be important resources for all individuals with developmental (and other) disabilities.

Mild Developmental Disability

Individuals with mild developmental disabilities compose about 85 percent of the population of individuals with developmental disabilities. Educational goals should focus on developing reading, writing, and other academic, social, and vocational skills to help the child assimilate as fully as possible into a typical adult life. A child with a mild developmental disability may display the following challenges:

- IQ of 55–69
- Reading ability up to seventh-grade level
- Requires some supervision and support
- Requires special education services
- Can be in regular school with special education services
- Considered "educable"
- May not be identified until second or third grade
- Employable and can be relatively independent as an adult

Moderate Developmental Disability

Individuals with moderate developmental disabilities make up about 10 percent of the population of individuals with developmental disabilities. Educational goals should focus on training the child to be as independent as possible as an adult. A child with a moderate developmental disability will display the following challenges:

- IQ of 35–54
- Considered "trainable"
- Difficulties with gross and fine motor coordination
- Needs a very structured classroom environment
- Generally taught in self-contained classrooms

- Will need more supervision later in life

- Can get jobs as an adult but usually very basic, unskilled ones

Severe Developmental Disability

Individuals with severe developmental disabilities make up about 3 percent of the population of individuals with developmental disabilities. The educational goal for the child with a severe developmental disability should be to teach activities of daily living (ADL) skills and survival skills. A child with a severe developmental disability will display the following challenges:

- IQ of 20–34

- Great difficulties with fine and gross motor coordination and speech

- Needs constant supervision

- Most likely must live in a group home or special school because of the extent of needs

Profound Developmental Disability

In addition to the challenges already described for a severe disability, the child with a profound developmental disability will display the following challenges:

- IQ of less than 20

- Limited, if any, speech

Educational goals should focus on developing the child's limited abilities as fully as possible, promoting inclusion, and ensuring a dignified quality of life.

Classroom Management Strategies

General Considerations

1. Plan several breaks throughout the school day. Tasks may drain this child more than other children his age.

2. Always respond to the child immediately and sincerely. When speaking to the child, face her so she can see you. Never speak with your back to her. If your back is turned to her, she may not recognize you are directing attention to her.

3. Assign jobs the child can succeed at to help him feel a sense of accomplishment (e.g., erasing the chalkboards).

4. Contrary to popular myth, many children with Down syndrome and other developmental disabilities have moderate to serious behavior problems. Work with the parents and the rest of the IEP team to develop a behavior plan that may be realistically applied at home and school, providing consistency.

5. Avoid shouting and using threats. The child will respond much better to positive reinforcement and praise than to strict tones of voice and harsh punishment techniques.

6. Be patient and know, understand, and remember the student's limits. Study the child's record and consult with the parents and educational team to help you best plan activities the child can learn from and excel at.

7. Systematically teach the child the importance of being on time to class and following the daily schedule; these concepts will likely be difficult for the child to grasp. For example, develop a "time clock" for the child to punch in on when she enters the classroom. This will help her become more aware of time and schedules and make her feel wanted and needed in the class. You may also encourage punctuality by scheduling a favorite activity first thing in the morning. This will motivate the child to come to school because she looks forward to starting the day with you.

8. Show the child how to keep a record of attendance and punctuality. Doing so fosters independent thinking as well as awareness of time passing over the course of the year.

9. Have the child sign a contract establishing the rewards and consequences for punctuality and tardiness. Be firm and fair, but above all, be very clear about what you expect concerning attendance and punctuality.

10. If the child is on a strict diet, know its limits and monitor what she is eating during snack time and lunchtime. Do not allow children to swap as in this case, it may be harmful. Stay alert!

Academic Considerations

11. Allow the child to look up the names of classmates' families in the phone book. If available, offer a smaller local guide.

12. Evaluate the length and level of each assignment to make sure it is within the ability level of the child. Design a series of short and simple, but more frequent, assignments. This will help the child gain self-confidence and build a foundation of success.

13. Build the curriculum specifically around the child's unique needs, abilities, and interests. Spend time talking with professionals and parents about what motivates and interests the child.

14. Use computer-assisted communication technology. Contact, or ask your special education staff to contact, your local assistive technology center for advice, demonstrations, and other support.

15. Evaluate the child periodically to make appropriate adjustments in your style of teaching. Consult with the other professionals in your school to determine what formal and informal assessment procedures have been or might be used.

16. Keep materials organized. Structure and organization provide an "anchor" to help guide the disorganized child.

17. Create assignments that help the child develop memory skills. Be patient, however, when teaching this skill because it is likely to be a big challenge for the child. Be prepared to repeat drills and other activities.

18. Design practice activities in any basic skill that relate well to the challenges the child faces in daily life. More specifically, develop activities that familiarize the child with menus, bus and train schedules, movie and television timetables, job advertisements, and the like. These will not only be fun for the child but will also be very practical and useful as she moves toward greater independence.

19. If safe, encourage the child to cook in school or at home to familiarize him with an important self-care skill and the concept of measurement. However, be very watchful, providing constant supervision.

20. If available, show the child how to buy something at the school store. Consider establishing a token economy through which he earns tokens for doing good work, then is allowed to buy certain items in the store.

21. Have the child collect food labels and compare the differences to learn about proper nutrition. Teach the child how to comparison shop.

22. Show the child how to budget her allowance (having found out from the parents what her allowance and allowed purchases are).

23. Make a chart on which the child records the daily temperature, fostering a greater awareness of the physical environment.

24. Provide the child with play money and a toy catalog, then have her "purchase" items and fill out the form.

25. Set up a messenger service in the classroom for the child to run, to motivate him to write messages and generally to communicate better with peers.

26. Involve the child in measuring the height of classmates.

27. Provide activities for older children that incorporate daily writing skills necessary for independence, such as filling out Social Security forms, driver's license applications, bank account applications, and so on.

28. To help the child see how to get organized, direct him to list the tasks to do for the day. If this is difficult for him, help him get started. Then, when the child completes what is on his list, let him check it off and reward him for doing a good job. If necessary, initially reward the child for completing each item on the list, then each two items, and so on, until he can complete a list before he receives a reward. This process will help him to see whether or not he is becoming more productive.

29. On a similar note, show the child how to use a daily planning book. This will further encourage independent organization and structure.

30. Use clocks, lists, and charts throughout the day. These are unemotional, concrete ways to let the child know what is expected in terms of time and responsibilities, offering strong structure and guidelines.

31. If necessary, use a language board for communication. For example, a simple language board may have four buttons on which you record four simple messages, one per button. The child learns to push the correct button to communicate her needs and wants to you. For example, one button might activate the recording, "I need to go to the bathroom." This helps the child learn that speech is a valuable tool while reducing some of the frustration she may feel with not being able to communicate well. The buttons may be different colors or have appropriate pictures attached. Again, contact your local assistive technology center for support.

32. Rewards don't all have to be things (e.g., stickers). Favorite activities, contingent upon successfully completing work, may be tremendous motivators. For example, if the child likes to kick the big red ball you have in the closet, arrange for him to

play with this ball at recess as a reward. Offer the reward activity as close to his performing the desired behavior as possible, then remind him why he is doing this special activity.

33. Make units thematic, integrated, and sequential, providing the student with the unifying structure he needs to assimilate and recall important information. For example, when teaching about trees, you might do a science lesson examining and identifying various trees' leaves, a writing lesson reporting about trees, and an art lesson drawing trees or taking bark rubbings.

34. Outdoor facilities and activities should encourage gross motor involvement so the child can gain better gross motor coordination.

35. Present instructions in small, sequential steps, and review each step frequently.

36. Focus reading assignments on learning how to gather information and on discovering the pleasure in reading as a leisure activity.

37. Design activities that encourage the child to become more aware of his surrounding environment. Take field trips to the local grocery store, hospital, post office, bakery, and the like to increase his familiarity with his community. Then have him list and/or report on each trip to reinforce the learning.

38. Provide and reinforce independent work, fostering independence from adult supervision.

39. Provide materials that are commensurate with the child's skill levels. Depending on the child's abilities, make sure these are as age-appropriate as possible. For example, a simple book on a favorite sport illustrated with pictures of teens or adults may be more interesting and therefore more motivating to a teenager than a first-grade book about two little boys getting a new puppy.

40. Repetition is critical. The child will need you to repeat things more than once to understand what you want.

41. Simplify lessons. Make them short and easy to help the student master what you are teaching, excel on tests, and feel good about his academic abilities.

42. Teach at a slower pace.

43. Never assume the child can move from point A to point C in learning without knowledge of point B.

44. Teach survival words (e.g., "danger," "warning," "poison") and words used every day.

45. To promote better decision-making skills, offer choices, then show the child how to make them. Initially, keep it simple, offering only two options at a time from which to choose. Progress to more complex choices if and when the child seems ready.

46. The more hands-on and demonstrative your lessons are, the better. Teach with real objects as much as possible, before using books and workbooks, then refer back to the real activities when using the written materials. Using the tree unit example, examine the parts of a real tree on the playground, then look at a poster identifying the parts of a tree.

47. Structure the classroom and general school environment so the child has access to the space, equipment, and materials she needs for optimal growth and development.

48. Use arts and crafts to help the child develop fine motor skills, eye-hand coordination, and social awareness. Such activities will encourage the child to work and share with others.

49. Teach with music if the child has an affinity for it. For example, teach the class a song about trees or have small groups make up songs to teach one another facts about trees.

50. When playing and interacting with the child, comment on surrounding objects and events to increase her vocabulary and her awareness of the environment.

Social Skills Development

51. Encourage interaction with nondisabled children. Foster group interaction, focusing on social skills. For example, include the child as part of a team that takes care of the class pets or does some other classroom chore. Calling it a "team" will help the child feel more connected to peers. Make sure the activities are geared to the child's abilities.

52. Along the same lines, assign the child a simple job that requires other students to go to her. For example, place her in charge of attendance, having her check off classmates' names as each reports in.

53. Encourage sports and other physical activities in and outside of school to deal with frustrations in a positive way and to decrease isolation.

54. Extend recess to help the child work through any frustrations.

55. Have the child participate in group activities that require sorting, pasting, addressing, folding, simple assembly, and so on.

56. Help the child start a hobby, then start a club for this hobby, involving other students.

57. Show the student how to develop friendships. For example, role-play approaching a person and introducing yourself.

58. Ask the school psychologist, school social worker, or other trained support staff member to develop and run a social skills group with the child and some classmates.

59. Recruit and train peer tutors for the child to help him establish relationships with his age peers.

Organizations

American Association on Mental Retardation (AAMR)
444 N. Capitol Street NW, Suite 846
Washington, DC 20001–1512
202–387–1968
800–424–3688 (outside the D.C. area)
Web site: www.aamr.org

The Arc (formerly the Association for Retarded Citizens of the
    United States)
1010 Wayne Avenue, Suite 650
Silver Spring, MD 20910
301–565–3842
800–433–5255
Web site: www.thearc.org
E-mail: info@thearc.org

National Down Syndrome Congress
7000 Peachtree-Dunwoody Road NE
Lake Ridge 400 Office Park
Building 5, Suite 100
Atlanta, GA 30328
770–604–9500
800–232–NDSC (800–232–6372)
Web site: www.ndsccenter.org
E-mail: NDSCcenter@aol.com

National Down Syndrome Society
666 Broadway
New York, NY 10012
212–460–9330
800–221–4602
Web site: www.ndss.org
E-mail: info@ndss.org

References and Bibliography

Berube, M. (1998). *Life as we know it: A father, a family, and an exceptional child.* New York: Random House.

Bierne-Smith, M., Ittenback, R., & Patton, J. R. (1998). *Mental retardation.* Old Tappan, NJ: Merrill.

Bogdan, R., & Taylor, S. J. (1994). *The social meaning of mental retardation.* New York: Teachers College Press.

Bray, N. M. (1997). *International review of research in mental retardation* (Vol. 20). San Diego: Academic.

Brill, M. T. (1993). *Keys to parenting a child with Down syndrome.* Hauppauge, NY: Barrons Educational.

Cicchetti, D., & Beeghly, M. (1995). *Children with Down syndrome: A developmental perspective.* Cambridge, MA: Brookline.

Cunningham, C. (1996). *Understanding Down syndrome: An introduction for parents.* Cambridge, MA: Brookline.

Dunbar, R. (1991). *Mental retardation.* New York: Venture.

Gibbs, B., & Spreinger, A. (1993). *Early use of total communication: Parents' perspectives on using sign language with young children with Down syndrome.* Baltimore: P. H. Brookes.

Gordon, M. A. (1998). *Let's talk about Down syndrome.* New York: Rosen.

Gunn, P., & Stratford, B. (1996). *New approaches to Down syndrome.* London: Cassell.

Hassold, T. J., & Patterson, D. (1998). *Down syndrome: A promising future, together.* New York: Wiley.

Jacobson, J. W., & Mulick, J. A. (1996). *Manual of diagnosis and professional practice in mental retardation.* Washington, DC: American Psychological Association.

Kliewer, C. (1998). *Schooling children with Down syndrome: Toward an understanding of possibility.* New York: Teachers' College Press.

Koch, J. H. (1997). *Robert Guthrie—the PKU story: Crusade against mental retardation.* Pasadena: Hope.

Kumin, L. (1994). *Communication skills in children with Down syndrome.* Rockville, MD: Woodbine.

McNey, M., & Fish, L. (1996). *Leslie's story: A book about a girl with mental retardation.* Minneapolis: Lerner.

Miller, J. F., Leavitt, L. A., & Leddy, M. (1998). *Improving the communication of people with Down syndrome.* Baltimore: P. H. Brookes.

Nugent, M. J. (1998). *Handbook on dual diagnosis.* Evergreen, CO: Mariah Management.

Olley, J. G., & Baroff, G. S. (1999). *Mental retardation: Nature, cause and management.* New York: Taylor and Francis.

Pueschel, S. M. (Ed.). (1990). *A parent's guide to Down syndrome: Toward a brighter future.* Baltimore: P. H. Brookes.

Pueschel, S. M. (1997). *Adolescents with Down syndrome: Toward a more fulfilling life.* Baltimore: P. H. Brookes.

Richardson, S. A., & Koller, H. (1997). *Twenty-two years: Causes and consequences of mental retardation.* Cambridge, MA: Brookline.

Selikowitz, M. (1997). *Down syndrome: The facts.* New York: Oxford University.

Smith, R. (1993). *Children with mental retardation: A parent's guide.* Rockville, MD: Woodbine.

Stallings, G., & Cook, S. (1998). *Another season: A coach's story of raising an exceptional son.* New York: Broadway.

Stratford, B., & Gunn, P. (1996). *New approaches to Down syndrome.* New York: Cassell.

Sumar, S. (1998). *Yoga for the special child: A therapeutic approach for infants and children with Down syndrome, cerebral palsy, and learning disabilities.* Buckingham, VA: Special Yoga.

Taylor, R. L. (1997). *Assessment of individuals with mental retardation.* San Diego: Singular.

Trainer, M. (1991). *Differences in common: Straight talk on mental retardation, Down syndrome, and life.* Rockville, MD: Woodbine.

Uhruh, J. F. (1994). *Down syndrome: Successful parenting of children with Down syndrome.* Eugene, OR: Fern Ridge.

U.S. Department of Education. (2000). *Twenty-second annual report to Congress on the implementation of the Individuals with Disabilities Education Act.* Washington, DC: Author.

CHAPTER 10

Pervasive Developmental Disorders/Autism

Definition

Pervasive developmental disorders (PDD) is a general term used to cover a number of more specific diagnoses: autistic disorder, Rett's disease, and Asperger's syndrome. These disorders share many of the same characteristics, and, of these, by far the most common is *autistic disorder.*

Autism is a neurological disorder that affects a child's ability to communicate, understand language, play, and relate to others. A diagnosis of autistic disorder is made when an individual displays six or more of twelve symptoms listed across three major areas: social interaction, communication, and behavior. When a child displays similar symptoms but does not meet the criteria for autistic disorder, the child may be diagnosed as having another form of PDD.

Autism is specifically covered under the IDEA. The IDEA defines *autism* as follows:

> Developmental disability significantly affecting verbal and nonverbal communication and social interaction, usually evident before age 3, that adversely affects a child's educational performance. Other characteristics associated with autism are engagement in repetitive activities and stereotyped movements, resistance to environmental change or change in daily routines, and unusual responses to sensory experiences.

Incidence

Autistic disorder occurs in 5 per 10,000 births, with reported rates ranging from 2 to 20 cases per 10,000 individuals. For unknown reasons, these disorders are four times more common in boys than girls. The causes are unknown. Currently, researchers are investigating various areas, including neurological damage and biochemical imbalance in the brain. Note, however, that these disorders are not caused by psychological factors.

Characteristics

Some or all of the following characteristics may be evident in mild to severe forms of autism and other forms of PDD:

- Apparent insensitivity to pain
- Avoidance of touching others
- Aggression
- Communication problems
- Difficulty relating to people
- Difficulty with changes in routine (insists on sameness)
- Absence of smiling at familiar people
- Echolalia (repeats words or phrases in place of normal language)
- Picky eating habits
- Hyper- or hyposensitive (over- or undersensitive)
- Inappropriate attachment to objects
- Inappropriate laughing and giggling
- Lack of imagination and inability to pretend
- Limited, if any, eye contact
- Limited range of interests
- Little interest in making friends
- Excessive concentration on a single item, idea, or person
- May not want cuddling
- Frequent tantrums for no apparent reason
- Apparent fearlessness

- Unresponsiveness to verbal cues (acts as if deaf)
- Noticeable physical overactivity or extreme sluggishness
- Pointing instead of using words
- Preference for being alone
- Repetitive behavior patterns
- Repetitive body movements
- Self-injurious behavior (e.g., head-banging)
- Spinning objects
- Sustained odd play
- Uneven gross and fine motor skills (one far superior to the other)
- Unresponsiveness to standard teaching methods
- Overreactive or underreactive responses to sensory information (e.g., loud noises, lights, certain textures of foods or fabrics)

Children with autism or other forms of PDD vary widely in abilities, intelligence, and behaviors. Some children do not speak, for example; others have limited language, often including repeated words or phrases. Individuals with more advanced language skills tend to talk about a limited range of topics and have difficulty understanding abstract concepts.

Educational Implications

Early diagnosis and appropriate educational programs are very important to children with autism or another form of PDD. The IDEA mandates that, from the age of 3, a child with autism is eligible for an educational program appropriate to his individual needs. Educational programs should focus on improving communication, social, academic, and behavioral skills as well as on developing activities of daily living (ADL) skills. Behavior and communication problems that interfere with learning sometimes require the involvement of a professional knowledgeable in the field of autism. This individual can develop and help implement an appropriate and coordinated plan for school staff and family to carry out at school and home, respectively.

In general, structure the classroom environment so the child's program is consistent, predictable, and therapeutic, helping the student learn better. In addition, presenting information both visually and verbally will help the student understand the material with less confusion along the way. Chances for interaction with nondisabled peers are also important because these students provide models of appropriate language, social, and behavioral skills. To overcome the common problem of the child's inability to automatically generalize skills learned at school to other environments, work with parents so learning activities, experiences, and approaches may be carried over into the home and community.

Because aggressive behavior can be a significant issue with the child with these difficulties, it is a good idea to be very clear about your school's policies with regard to restraint. Find out what procedures are to be followed and whom to call upon for help if it becomes necessary. There are ways to restrain a child without hurting him (e.g., therapeutic crisis intervention).

Even faced with these challenges, with educational programs designed to meet their needs and specialized adult support services in employment and living arrangements, these children can, as adults, live and work productively.

Classroom Management Techniques

General Considerations

1. Help the child pay attention because he is likely to have great difficulty staying on task and maintaining a focus for a long period of time.

2. Help the child learn to make choices as these difficult situations arise. Initially, offer only two choices at a time.

3. Be very clear and organized with everything you teach and do, especially when giving instructions. Any confusion will only create further anxiety, conflict, and tension for both you and the student.

4. Work to guide the child toward independence, decreasing her reliance on adults. Foster independent academic, social, emotional, and life skills.

5. Establish routine patterns: *Spatial routines* associate specific locations with specific activities—for example, a pictorial chart used as a daily schedule. *Temporal routines* associate time with an activity and make the beginning and ending of an activity visually evident. *Instructional routines* associate specific social and communication behaviors.

6. Beyond routines, keep classroom rules, arrangement, and other factors consistent and predictable. The child is likely to feel very uncomfortable with change in any form. He needs to feel secure by learning that, at all times, the classroom is a stable, reliable place with stable, reliable teachers and other caregivers.

7. Learn not to become frustrated or turned off by unappealing or inappropriate conduct. Simply expect certain behaviors to present themselves, accepting your responsibility as a professional to handle them matter-of-factly as they arise.

8. Keep the student active and involved to help prevent stereotypic behaviors (e.g., rocking) from occurring. Do not give the student time to begin an inappropriate behavior.

9. Initiate one-on-one interactions frequently throughout the day to help increase the child's eye contact.

Academic Considerations

10. Use positive reinforcement rather than punishment to get your points across. The child will respond much better to reward and praise than to lecturing or other negative forms of discipline.

11. Break tasks down into simple parts. This will help the child achieve greater success while avoiding unnecessary frustration.

12. Constantly test to see whether or not the child has progressed sufficiently to try something new. Consult with the various professionals within the school to find out what types of formal and informal testing have already been done and what may be done periodically to evaluate progress.

13. Consciously teach the child to identify colors and shapes and learn the process of matching pictures to actual objects.

14. Repeat, repeat, repeat instructions to help the child stay focused on the task at hand.

15. Keep activities interesting and varied. As with all children, the more interesting and varied the curriculum, the greater the chance the child will be motivated to complete work and try to succeed.

16. Present information both verbally and visually to improve understanding.

17. Enhance the child's understanding of instructional and environmental structure by providing routines and visual aids in forms other than written language. For example, learn a few American Sign Language signs to signal transitions, such as the sign for food for snack or lunchtime.

18. Activities must be well-organized. Structure each lesson with great care and thought. For example, give out materials only as the student needs to use them.

19. Likewise, minimize time waiting to begin activities. Have all materials prepared and handy when starting the lesson. Teaching that is "scattered" and disorganized upsets the child with autism or other forms of PDD.

Social Skills Development

20. Teach appropriate social skills through modeling behavior and role-playing. Remember, however, to be patient, repeatedly taking the time to help the child learn how to act in various situations. Expending this effort can be difficult, especially if the disability is severe, but it will pay off.

21. Privately help the child role-play, with another student, a problematic social situation, so she can get feedback from a peer.

22. As you have the child role-play various social situations over time, help him create a "toolbox" of responses and options for typical social situations. An index card file and index cards on which, situation by situation, you or the child writes the tools he has practiced is a powerful teaching method. Encourage the child to review frequently what behaviors worked in which situations.

23. Speak with school support staff or a community mental health care provider or center about including the child in a social skills development group. This may be difficult, however, if the disability is severe.

24. Arrange for a peer to guide and cue the child through social situations. The child may be more willing to model her own behavior after peer behavior than she would to model it after an adult's.

25. Incorporate small, intensive group lessons.

26. Initially, keep groups small for the child, assigning only one reliable and patient peer partner. Gradually increase the size of the group as the child becomes more comfortable and socially adept.

27. Design goal-oriented group projects on which students must work together to accomplish a task (e.g., each child must research one part of an assigned topic to complete the project, then report findings to the others). Remember, initially limit this to the student and one other child.

28. Allow the child and a responsible peer partner to organize team activities or group projects. The child may rise to the occasion when placed in a leadership role.

29. When the child is refraining from exhibiting aggressive or inappropriate social behavior, praise him as often as you can do so realistically and genuinely. Catch him displaying the target positive behaviors.

30. The child may not understand what may seem to you to be social common sense because of the disability or a lack of experience. Therefore, initially, take a more direct approach to teaching social skills rather than allowing the child to learn through trial and error. Specifically, the child may need help interpreting social situations and developing appropriate responses. For example, you might help the child understand how to take turns with a toy.

31. Many children with autism or PDD do not understand appropriate greetings and gestures. Practice these every day so they become routine to the child. Once the child learns to greet a classmate, with or without your cueing, the classmate may be distracted by the noise the rest of the class is making and not respond, leading the child to conclude that the attempt at communication was ineffective, or worse, that the classmate now "hates" him. You can correct such erroneous thinking by simply cueing the child to try to greet the classmate again, briefly explaining why the other child may not have responded initially: "It was too noisy for Steven to hear you. Try saying 'Hello' again."

Communication Considerations

32. The complexity of messages you give should match the child's level of comprehension. Therefore, be very knowledgeable of the cognitive level of the child. Since IQ can vary tremendously, it is critical to know what is reasonable versus what is not possible in regard to academic performance.

33. Drill the child on communication skills intensively. The speech and language therapist in your school should be able to provide these for you and the parents to reinforce. Remember, the student will need special help to develop communication skills. Look beyond standard methods of developing verbal skills to using augmentative communication systems, such as American Sign Language.

34. To this end, facilitate communication whenever possible through assistive technology devices (e.g., talking computer software, communication boards). Contact your local assistive technology center for strategy ideas, product demonstrations, and other supports, including funding.

Organizations

Autism Hotline
Autism Services Center
P.O. Box 507
Pritchard Building, 605 Ninth Street
Huntington, WV 25710–0507
304–525–8014

Autism National Committee
249 Hampshire Drive
Plainsboro, NJ 08536

Autism Society of America
7910 Woodmont Avenue, Suite 300
Bethesda, MD 20814–3015
301–657–0881
800–3AUTISM (800–328–8476)
Web site: www.autism-society.org

Institute for the Study of Developmental Disabilities
Indiana Resource Center for Autism
Indiana University
2853 East 10th Street
Bloomington, IN 47408–2696
812–855–6508
TTY: 812–855–9396
Web site: www.iidc.indiana.edu
E-mail: foshaj@indiana.edu

References and Bibliography

Aarons, M., & Gittens, T. (1992). *The handbook of autism: A guide for parents and professionals.* New York: Routledge.

Autism Society of America. (1996). *What is autism?* Bethesda: Author.

Brill, M. T. (1994). *Keys to parenting the child with autism.* New York: Barrons Educational Services.

Cohen, D. J., & Volkmar, F. R. (1997). *Handbook of autism and pervasive developmental disorders.* New York: Wiley.

Dawson, G. (1999). *Autism: Nature, diagnosis, and treatment.* New York: Guilford.

Dillon, K. M. (1995). *Living with autism: The parents' stories.* Boone, NC: Parkway.

Gerlach, E. K. (1998). *Autism treatment guide.* Eugene, OR: Four Leaf.

Happe, F. (1998). *Autism: An introduction to psychological theory.* Cambridge, MA: Brookline.

Harris, S. L. (1994). *Siblings of children with autism: A guide for families.* Bethesda: Woodbine.

Harris, S. L., & Weiss, M. J. (1998). *Right from the start: Behavioral intervention for young children with autism—A guide for parents and professionals.* Bethesda: Woodbine.

Hart, C.A. (1993). *A parent's guide to autism: Answers to the most common questions.* New York: Simon & Schuster.

Journal of Autism and Developmental Disorders. Available from Plenum Publishing, 233 Spring Street, New York, NY 10013; 800–221–9369.

Kogel, R. (1995). *Teaching children with autism: Strategies for initiating positive interactions and improving learning opportunities.* Baltimore: P. H. Brookes.

Maurice, C., Green, G., & Luce, S. C. (Eds.). *Behavioral intervention for young children with autism: A manual for parents and professionals.* Austin, TX: PRO-ED.

McClannahan, L. E., & Krantz, P. J. (1999). *Activity schedules for children with autism: Teaching independent behavior.* Bethesda: Woodbine.

Mesibov, G. B., & Adams, L. W. (1998). *Autism: Understanding the disorder.* New York: Plenum.

New Jersey Center for Outreach and Services for the Autism Community (COSAC). (1994, December). *National directory of programs serving individuals with autism and related pervasive developmental disorders.* Available from the author, 1450 Parkside Avenue, Suite 22, Ewing, NJ 08638; 609–883–8100.

Powers, M. D. (Ed.). (1989). *Children with autism: A parent's guide.* Bethesda, MD: Woodbine.

Sigman, M., & Capps, L. (1997). *Children with autism: A developmental perspective.* Cambridge, MA: Brookline.

CHAPTER 11

Giftedness

Definition

A *gifted* child is one who shows or has the potential for an exceptional level of performance in one or more areas of expression. Some of these abilities are very general, affecting a broad spectrum of the child's life (e.g., leadership skills or creative thinking). Some are very specific talents, only evident in certain circumstances (e.g., special aptitude in mathematics, science, or music). *Giftedness* is a general term referring to this spectrum of abilities.

Incidence

A total of 3 to 5 percent of the school population are considered gifted or talented.

Characteristics

Characteristics that describe a gifted child may include the following:

- Advanced ability to make moral judgments
- Highly alert
- Extremely curious intellectually
- Quickly bored in a classroom designed for average children
- Well-organized behavior and thinking
- Ability to break down difficult problems into basic components
- High aptitude for critical thinking

- Very self-critical
- Consistently scores in top 10 percent on achievement tests
- High level of creativity and inventiveness
- Diverse interests and abilities
- Independent in work, study, and other activities
- Enjoys challenges
- Enjoys going to school and learning new things
- Very expressive
- Flexible thinker
- Reads at a young age (i.e., before entering school)
- Goal-oriented
- Great power of concentration
- Boundless sense of energy; high energy level
- Develops creative solutions to social and environmental problems
- Adept at conceptualizing ideas
- High self-confidence
- Takes great pleasure in intellectual activities
- Unusual interest in cause-and-effect relationships
- High interest in inductive learning and problem solving
- Loves reading
- Intrinsically motivated
- Keen powers of observation
- Large vocabulary and strong verbal skills
- Prefers company of older children
- Refuses to simply accept what an authority says
- Needs freedom of movement and action
- Very capable of understanding and proposing abstract ideas
- Prefers individualized work
- Questioning attitude
- Responds and relates well to parents, teachers, and other adults

- Excellent memory
- Self-reliant
- Self-motivated
- Sets realistic goals, then works to accomplish them
- Strong and mature sense of humor
- Strong leadership skills
- Strong perseverance
- Unusual emotional depth and intensity
- Very good observational skills
- Wide range of experiences and knowledge
- Willingness to explore the unusual (things, ideas)

Educational Implications

Be aware that gifted children will become easily bored if not academically and creatively stimulated. It is worth the effort when you see the gifted child moving toward her full potential. Two main types of programs should be included in the gifted child's curriculum: enrichment programs and acceleration programs. Enrichment programs may involve any of the following:

- Alternative schools
- Extra-school activities
- Field trips and cultural programs
- Guest speakers
- Internships
- Mentor programs
- Minicourses
- Pull-out programs
- Resource room access
- Seminars
- Special clubs
- Special experiences within a regular classroom
- Grouping with other gifted children in the regular classroom

- Self-contained gifted classrooms
- Summer camps and programs
- Team teaching

Acceleration programs may take any of the following forms:

- Honors classes
- Advanced placement classes for college credit
- Advanced placement tests
- Continuous progress curricula
- Correspondence courses
- Credit by examination
- Early admission to elementary school
- Skipping a grade
- Early admission to college
- Extra classes for extra credit
- Flexible scheduling
- Independent study
- Multiage classes
- Programmed learning, allowing the student to accelerate at his own pace
- Seminars
- Tutoring younger students
- Ungraded classes
- Year-round school

Classroom Management Strategies

General Considerations

1. Pick up the pace of learning. The gifted student needs to have academic curriculum move at a more rapid pace to stay interested and motivated.

2. Broaden the range of experiences. Give the child more opportunities to expand her horizons, as already suggested under "Educational Implications."

3. Give the child challenging problems. He may enjoy and take pride in figuring out complex, detailed situations.

4. Create cooperative projects and problems that call for more creative thought and critical thinking (e.g., challenge the child with open-ended questions for which no correct answer exists). She will enjoy trying to solve such problems (e.g., "If you were on a sinking boat with a group of other people and could only save one of them, how would you decide whom to save?").

5. Allow the student to pursue individual projects that require sophisticated levels of thinking. She will enjoy working on her own, so encourage her to do so. Challenge her and avoid giving away answers.

6. Participate in professional organizations that enhance your knowledge about ways to reach the gifted child. Become well-prepared and well-versed in how to teach and motivate the child.

7. Teach the child how to play chess, the ideal game for the gifted child because it requires great skill, concentration, and strategic planning.

8. Encourage the student to participate actively in various events that emphasize particular skills or knowledge areas ("mathletics," debate team, chess club). This will foster greater awareness of chances for community service.

9. Let the child chair class committees, direct plays, or assume other active peer-leadership roles. This will not only use the child's many strengths but will also help the child develop any social skills that are lacking.

10. Let the child know you care about his progress. Do not avoid him or pay limited attention to him simply because he is more gifted than the other children. Like any other child, he needs attention and praise.

11. Specifically, don't crush a gifted child's enthusiasm by not calling on him. Since he may often know most of the answers faster than the other children, you may have a tendency to get discouraged or annoyed by so-called show-off tendencies. Instead, establish the idea with the child early on that you will call on him but not all the time.

12. Don't ask the child to do repetitive, rote tasks. This will bore her and create hostility and frustration for both of you.

13. Don't repress creativity by rejecting an unusual idea. The "crazy" idea may actually have some merit. Let the child try to expand her horizons, and teach her how to brainstorm and share her ideas in appropriate ways.

14. Don't ask the child to tutor others for excessive lengths of time. While this approach may be very tempting, do not lose sight of the fact that this child is a student who needs to use most of his time to excel and reach his own potential, not to help others. When you do have him tutor other students, focus on developing his own social skills more fully, not just on the other students' academic needs.

Academic Considerations

15. Incorporate activities that encourage original, fluent, and flexible thinking into the child's curriculum. Example challenges include the following: "Think of new ways to use a matchbox or write a new ending to a famous play"; "List all the things you can fit through a hole the size of a penny, or name all the things you can pin up with a thumbtack. Design a way to test your ideas"; "Think of all the ways you can use items in your garbage can to reduce pollution"; "Explain how life would be different if electricity had not been discovered."

16. Likewise, design complex assignments to elicit elaborate thinking: "Draw a pentagon, and make as many objects as you can that include that shape"; "Expand on the safety items for airplanes that have already been developed"; "Develop solutions to stop school violence"; or "If teachers didn't assign grades, propose what should be used to determine how a student is doing in school."

17. Expose the student to problems that spark his curiosity and imagination: "Describe what would happen if, all of a sudden, you became totally deaf"; "Describe what you think the world would be like without the sun"; or "Suppose Martians landed on the earth, and all they found was a penny. How many things would they be able to tell about our society from that penny? Explain your reasoning."

18. Assign tasks that encourage the child to take risks in her thinking—for example, "How would you go about finding out what an object in a paper bag is if you couldn't see it?" or "Explain how you would defend Napoleon if you were his lawyer."

Organizations

American Association for Gifted Children
1121 W. Main Street
Durham, NC 27701
919–783–6152

Council for Exceptional Children
1920 Association Drive
Reston, VA 22091–1589
703–620–3660
888–CEC–SPED (888–232–7733; toll-free)
Web site: www.cec.sped.org
E-mail: service@cec.sped.org

National Association for Gifted Children
1707 L Street NW, Suite 550
Washington, DC 20036
202–785–4268
Web site: www.nagc.org
E-mail: request@nagc.org

References and Bibliography

Baldwin, A. Y., & Vialle, W. (1998). *The many faces of giftedness: Lifting the mask.* Albany, NY: Delmar.

Clark, B. (1992). *Growing up gifted.* Columbus, OH: Merrill.

Davis, G., & Rimm, S. (1994). *Education of the gifted and talented.* Englewood Cliffs, NJ: Prentice Hall.

Esquirel, G. B., & Houtz, J. C. (1999). *Creativity and giftedness in culturally diverse students.* Cresskill, NJ: Hampton.

Friedman, R. C., & Rogers, K. B. (1998). *Talent in context: Historical and social perspectives on giftedness.* Washington, DC: American Psychological Association.

Kent, D., & Quinlan, K. A. (1997). *Extraordinary people with disabilities.* Danbury, CT: Children's Press.

Kerr, B. A. (1997). *Smart girls: A new psychology of girls, women, and giftedness.* Scottsdale, AZ: Gifted Psychological Press.

Li, R. (1996). *A theory of conceptual intelligence: Thinking, learning, creativity, and giftedness.* Westport, CT: Greenwood.

Maker, C. J., & King, M. A. (1996). *Nurturing giftedness in young children.* Reston, VA: Council for Exceptional Children.

Streznewski, M. K. (1999). *Gifted grownups: The mixed blessing of extraordinary potential.* New York: Wiley.

Winner, E. (1997). *Gifted children: Myths and realities.* New York: Basic.

About the Authors

Dr. Roger Pierangelo is a New York State licensed clinical psychologist. He has years of experience as a regular classroom teacher, school psychologist, and administrator of psychology programs. He has served as full professor in the graduate Special Education Department at Long Island University; member of various committees on special education; evaluator for the New York State Education Department; director of a private clinic; and consultant to numerous private and public schools, PTAs, and SEPTA groups.

Dr. Pierangelo earned his B.S. from St. John's University, M.S. and professional diploma from Queens College, and Ph.D. from Yeshiva University. He is a member of the American Psychological Association, New York State Psychological Association, Nassau County Psychological Association, New York State Union of Teachers, and Phi Delta Kappa.

Dr. Pierangelo is the author of numerous books, including *The Survival Kit for the Special Education Teacher* and *The Special Education Teacher's Book of Lists* (Simon and Schuster), and *301 Ways to Be a Loving Parent* and *The World's Most Provocative Questions* (SPI Publishers). He is coauthor of *The Parent's Guide to Special Education, The Complete Guide to Transition Services,* and *The Special Educator's Complete Guide to 109 Diagnostic Tests* (Simon and Schuster); *The Special Education Yellow Pages* (Merrill); *Assessment in Special Education* (Allyn and Bacon); and *Why Your Students Do What They Do and What to Do When They Do It (Grades K–5* and *Grades 6–12;* Research Press).

Dr. George A. Giuliani is a full-time assistant professor of psychology at St. Joseph's College in Patchogue, New York. He is a New York State licensed clinical psychologist and a member of the New York Association of School Psychologists and the National Association of School Psychologists.

Dr. Giuliani earned his B.A. from the College of the Holy Cross, M.S. from St. John's University, J.D. from City University Law School, and Psy.D. from The Graduate School of Applied and Professional Psychology at Rutgers University.

Dr. Giuliani is coauthor of *The Special Educator's Complete Guide to 109 Diagnostic Tests* (Simon and Schuster); *Assessment in Special Education* (Allyn and Bacon); and *Why Your Students Do What They Do and What to Do When They Do It* (*Grades K–5* and *Grades 6–12*; Research Press).